The Evolution of Bid Whist

150 Years in the Growth of an African American Tradition

by

Ronald L. Allen

Life To Legacy, LLC

The Evolution of Bid Whist:
150 Years in the of Growth of an
Afriacn American Tradition

By: Ronald L. Allen

ISBN-10: 1939654-8-0
ISBN-13: 978-1-9396543-8-0

Printed in the United States

10 9 8 7 6 5 4 3 2 1

Cover Design and interior layout by:
Ronald L. Allen

Published by:
Life To Legacy, LLC
P.O. Box 57
Blue Island, IL 60406
www.Life2Legacy.com

Presented to:

To contact the author send email to:
Bidwhistpros@gmail.com

DEDICATION

I dedicate this book to all Bid Whist players who are passionate about the game. I have played across the country for over fifty-five years and participated in several major tournaments. Bid Whist affords many exciting hours of fun and entertainment for the young and old. People who genuinely enjoy the game will spend fourtoeight hours in a day engaged in this fun experience.

During my teenage years, Bid Whist provided me with an outlet and an alternative to being involved in gang activity. I wish to thank Mrs. Emma Prince for allowing our group to play Bid Whist in her home. Mrs. Prince had two daughters, Reatha and Gwendolyn, and she opened her home to teenagers to provide a safe environment for young adults. Mrs. Prince's loving patience converted a collection of potential street urchins into an off-the-street band of friends. Our group stayed in school and went on to achieve successful careers because we had a fun alternative to the lure of the dangerous streets of Chicago.

It was not an easy task because she sacrificed many quiet moments by having a bunch of teenagers in her house four or five days a week. I acknowledge with sincere gratitude that her strategy was a success. Mrs. Prince required that we be polite at all times and maintain respect for their home and each guest. The fun-filled moments at the Prince home taught us to be good citizens. None of the kids who played cards at the Prince residence was ever involved in criminal activities, and we all safely reached adulthood, while honing our skills at playing the great game of Bid Whist.

Bid Whist is an enduring cultural artifact of the African American community. My strong desire to preserve this heritage for posterity motivated my efforts to capture all available information on this subject and share it with anyone desiring to know the complete history. The history of Bid Whist shared in this book will address the myths and offer a deeper insight into how the game originated. Some of the chapters offer strategies and techniques for players to improve their winning percentages.

INTRODUCTION

The authors of previous books on Bid Whist did an excellent job describing the generalities of the game, but, in my opinion, some relevant granular questions remained unanswered.

This book is more than an instruction manual; it is a chronicle of the long and rich heritage of Bid Whist. The book's history section offers little known information which will give readers a greater appreciation of the game. I address many unanswered questions as I show the cultural connection between Bid Whist and notable people and moments in history.

Bid Whist is a card game that originated in the U.S. and is similar to the games of Whist, Bridge, and Spades. Bid Whist has an expanded bidding format that requires a different strategic approach than the other games. In the past, primarily African Americans played Bid Whist, but today many nationalities enjoy the game. Over twenty-five million people play Bid Whist across the globe.

Bid Whist started near the end of slavery and traveled with African American soldiers in every military engagement since the Civil War. The game of Bid Whist has lasted through the Industrial Revolution, the Great Depression, the Civil Rights Movement, and the struggle for Gay Rights. Since Bid Whist began, the mode of transportation has gone from horses to cars, to trains, to airplanes and space travel. The game has traversed time from

President Abraham Lincoln to the first African American President, Barack Obama.

The legacy of Bid Whist is more than its long history and unique playing strategies. It is a cultural quilt made up of patches of our African American history, and each patch interwoven in the quilt represents a significant segment of the Black journey in America. A comprehensive history of Bid Whist must include the cultural relationships represented in these patches and their impact upon our community. This book focuses on the connection between Bid Whist and the Black community.

TABLE OF CONTENTS

SECTION I—HISTORY

SECTION II—RULES & GAME STRATEGIES

SECTION I

History

CHAPTER ONE
The History of Bid Whist

The introduction of this book states that the game of Bid Whist has strong ties to the African American community. Although Bid Whist originated in the Black community, it currently has spread across the globe and today exists in many nations. Winston Churchill stated, "The farther backward you can look, the farther forward you are likely to see." This quote reminded me of the symbolism of the Sankofa Bird in African culture.[1] This metaphor was a directive that I should begin with the deepest possible inspection of the history of Bid Whist.

This book is more than an instructional guide, and the first section contains a comprehensive study of the rich heritage of Bid Whist and its continuing bond with the African-American community. It shares little-known items of cultural interest that may

[1] The Sankofa Bird looks backward with the egg of the future in her beak, constantly checking as she moves into the future.

appear disparate, but these items clarify how Bid Whist had a continuous interconnection with millions of Black people.

My initial research revealed that during the nineteenth century and most of the twentieth century, many historians deemed Afrocentric historical facts insignificant. This resulted in important pieces of African American history not being captured in printed materials. Possibly, this made historians reluctant to offer a conclusive statement that Blacks originated Bid Whist. This book offers a preponderance of the evidence to show that the slave community in America took segments from Whist and Bridge and developed Bid Whist.

Throughout American history, many African American ideas and inventions have been stolen and attributed to European-Americans. There is strong evidence that similar hijacking attempts are now in progress concerning the game of Bid Whist. My concern in this area prompted me to begin a historical research of the game. I investigated the period when the game of Whist evolved into Bid Whist, and I found only a few books written about Whist. Because of the cultural climate during that era, there were no books written that addressed Bid Whist specifically.

Although there were a few books published by Black authors during that time, one book was published as early as 1853. Those few books described the struggles and injustices faced by Black people. The humanitarian relevancy of racial injustice was an important subject matter, and many liberal Whites wanted to learn more about it. These books focused on increasing public awareness and garnered support from sympathetic Whites. However, information on Bid Whist had little marketable value, and publishers viewed the printing of such a book as a bad business decision. Whites did not play bid Whist, and publishers were reluctant to print books with little marketability, especially any books focusing on a card game that was the source of enjoyment only for Black people.

This thorough examination of the background history of the game and its rules will accomplish two goals. The first goal is to validate and preserve this important part of our African American culture for posterity. I attempt to do this with a thorough documentation of existing written materials and personal interviews with contemporary players and senior members of our community who can best remember the origins and core of the game's initial playing components. I believe the Black community should afford this game "landmark" status. Any idea or creation that continues to exist for 150 years should be worthy of special recognition. Bid Whist is one of our cultural traditions, and the Black community should not allow distortion of the game's history.

The second goal is to capture the game's original make-up and dispel many of the myths and inaccuracies displayed on Internet sites on the subject. These errors distort the true history of the game. This book shares additional historical background on the game and offers reasonable substantiation of the information, which may support and encourage further research by interested readers.

The Resources used for Research

I researched the game of Bid Whist using all the resources currently available. I visited major libraries across the nation, including the Library of Congress in Washington, DC, and I reviewed the related subject material on hand in these institutions. The emergence of the Internet and email communications allowed me to develop relationships with players who played Bid Whist in other countries. People play Bid Whist and its hybrid forms in Great Britain, France, Spain, Italy, Norway, Sweden, Australia, Finland, Canada, Iceland, South Africa, and other nations. When language barriers permitted, I took the opportunity to learn about how and when the people of these countries began to play this game.

My comprehensive research consisted of personal interviews, Internet research, online surveys, newspaper archives, and the vast resources of museums. I researched the files of several libraries, including the European Library, the National Library of Paris, and the Library of Congress. I only found five books devoted entirely to Bid Whist in the European libraries, and American authors wrote them all. In the United States, I researched many books published on Whist, Bridge, and their predecessors. I reconstructed the ancestry of each game to explore the metamorphosis of possible games that may have parented Bid Whist. However, I found there was a void in published books on Bid Whist before the late 1900s. I established the existence of the game during that phase through college newspapers, excerpts from diaries, personal recounting, and mentions in Afrocentric books on other subjects. Even so, Bid Whist remained hidden underground. Bid Whist's history was similar to liquor during Prohibition; you knew it was out there, but you had to locate the "speakeasy."

I contacted the Amtrak Corp. and enlisted their help in identifying the Pullman porters who are currently alive. I contacted some of those still living and spoke to them about their recollections of the game during the early 1900s. This interview process was an enjoyable experience but very challenging because many of the living members were in their eighties and nineties. The senior years of those surviving porters presented occasional challenges related to hearing difficulties, loss of memory, and other expected health issues for people of their age.

I interviewed grandparents and great-grandparents during this process because I wanted to learn the roots of Bid Whist. This was a very pleasant experience because I met some wonderful people and heard many colorful stories.

The data gathered from the diaries of our centenarians and supercentenarians was an invaluable source of validating information. I learned that researching Bid Whist was as difficult as researching Black genealogy back past the early 1800s. There was very little published information on Bid Whist before 1900, and there were no books on this subject written by a Black author until the twentieth century.

I conducted surveys of Bid Whist players across the country. I attempted to identify existing players and the people that originally taught the game to these current players. I wanted to capture how the game has passed from generation to generation in the U.S., and to use this information to trace the evolution of the game.[2] Information results from the last survey revealed:

• 28% of current players started playing when they were under sixteen years old.

• 89% prefer to play with a six-card Kitty.

• 63% have been playing more than twenty years.

• 53% currently play at least five days a week.

• 32% learned to play in the Midwest; the Southeast and Northeast tied at 26.3%.

• 68% of current players consider themselves very competitive players.

The absence of information providing a clear path to follow prompted me to map a different search process. I used a method accepted at most graduate business colleges to identify the seven stages in the life cycle of a new idea. Graduate schools recognize the following steps in the evolution cycle:

---

[2] (2013 Survey of 784 Bid Whist Players conducted through Survey Monkey)

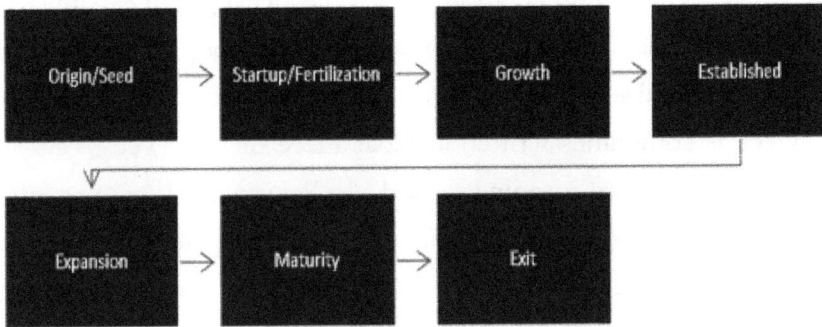

The Search for the Origin of Bid Whist

Most historians appeared to agree that Bid Whist's origins would have started with the game of Whist. This assertion became the starting point of my search, and I looked for contradictions to this premise. Most available printed materials coincide with the writings of Alice Howard Cady, who states, Whist began with the English game of Triumph, and its earlier variants—Ruff & Honours, Slamm, and Whisk[3]—appeared in the early 1500s.[4] These games were also members of the Whist family. The twentieth-century offshoots of Whist are Bridge, Auction Bridge, Contract Bridge, Minnesota, Classic, Bid 52, Spades, and Bid Whist. Individual cultures incorporated preferential modifications to the Whist game. The examination of the game of Whist offered the most accurate insight into the creation of Bid Whist.

---

[3] In 1520, there was a variant of the game that was spelled Whisk.

[4] (Cady, 1895)

There is documentation of people playing games similar to Whist in Asia. These games, which were very popular in India and Pakistan, had several names. Ms. Cady also states, The name Court Piece is sometimes written as Coat Piece or Coat Pees, Pees being a Hindi word meaning to deal. In Pakistan, this game is often known as Rang, which means trump. In some places, for example, in Goa, it is called Seven Hands. In India, the English word hand is used to mean a trick - i.e. a set of cards, one played by each player in turn.

The word Court, Coat, Kot or Kout occurs in many South Asian games as far away as Somalia and Malaysia. It usually means something like a slam, a situation in which one team wins all the tricks or at least a succession of tricks, while the other team wins none.[5] The origin of the word Kot is unclear, but one writer, Thierry Depaulis,[6] suggests that it may perhaps have come from Tamil or some other Dravidian language. Another school of thought believes that card playing originated in China, as that country invented paper and probably produced the first paper cards. This theory is quite logical, as we know that there were many earlier card games in Asia. I also found many examples of playing cards used in other countries prior to the sixteenth century.

15th century Islamic cards: king of coins and 5 of polo sticks

---

[5] (Cady, 1895)
[6] *A Wicked Pack of Cards:* Thierry Depaulis

Written references show Whist played in Greece, Egypt, and the French Riviera in the mid-1800s. In 1894, Whist returned strongly in London. I explored the history of where the game originated, and I found references that one of the greatest Whist players of the 1800s was a Frenchman, M. Deschapelles. Mr. Edmond Hoyle[7] mentions the game of Cayenne, which was an early French game that many believed inspired the features in Bid Whist so that the dealer could make the trump or pass the privilege to his partner.[8]

There is no consensual agreement of the origin of Whist. However, in England in the seventeenth century, Whist was well known and most sophisticated people knew the game. A group of men who frequented the Crown Coffee House in Bedford Row, London, around 1728, first played Whist on scientific principles. Edmund Hoyle was a member of this group. Some believe that Whist originated in Turkey and was adopted by the British, who brought it to the United States during their occupancy of our country.

Personally, I tend to disbelieve this school of thinking because the game has no structural elements that reflect a Turkish flavor in either the pictorial images or language used in the game. My research of the games in Turkey uncovered only one game that would be similar to Whist—Maca Kizi—a game comparable to

---

[7] Edmond Hoyle (1672-1769) was an author best known for his books on the rules and play of card games. He remains the world's most recognized authority on card games. The phrase according to Hoyle" remains in use today.

[8] (Hoyle, 1743)

Hearts. There should have been remnants reflecting the cultural heritage if the game were imported from Turkey. There was nothing in the Turkish writings or within the game itself to reflect their culture. My research did not find any written materials to support this claim. It is possible someone read the general history of card playing and mistakenly transferred that history into the playing of Whist.

Most experts believe that the Whist game originated in England or France, with the majority citing its birth in England. The writings of one author, Mr. Cavendish, stated that scholars returning from studying in England introduced the game in France.[9] The pictorial design of playing cards indicate that the country of origin would have been a monarchy; thus, the ranking card characters were Kings and Queens who exercised dominance over the lower cards.

European-style playing cards arrived in Europe somewhere from 1360 to 1379.[10] In the sixteenth century, Rouen, a city in France, was a major producer of playing cards. Each King in their deck of playing cards represented a person recognized in history as a great King. They assigned representative names to the King cards in the deck:[11]

---

[9] *The Laws and Principles of Whist* by "Cavendish", John Wurtle Lovell; New York; 1880; pp. 43-64.
[10] (A Brief History of Playings Cards, 2007)
[11] The Suburban Woman of DuPage County July 15, 2012 & www. blurit.com

The King of Spades - King David

The King of Hearts - Charlemagne

The King of Clubs - Alexander the Great

The King of Diamonds - Julius Caesar

Whist appeared in England sometime in the sixteenth century as a hybrid of Ruff and Honours & Trump. The game spread to the court of Louis XV in France around 1710. It was later spread to America in the 1700s by immigrating settlers. There is documented evidence that many of our country's ancestors played Whist, including George Washington, Benjamin Franklin, and Thomas Jefferson, among other notables.[12]

In the seventeenth century, many of the more educated people and people of influence began to talk about and play the game. There were scattered references that alluded to Whist being played by "people under the stairs" or within other unfinished/unused portions of the plantation owner's mansion. The term was a polite reference to the cramped living quarters allotted to the Black house slaves and servants. In 1743, Hoyle published *A Short Treatise on Whist*.[13] Whist became the card game that was widely played in circles of intellectuals in the English-speaking countries until supplanted by its offspring, Bridge. Some who played against Mr. Hoyle have spoken of him as a third-rate card player. However, Hoyle was a careful observer and writer. These traits established

---

[12] http://www.whistonline.net/whist_history.html
[13] (Hoyle, 1743)

him as an authority. Hoyle may not have been a skilled card player, but he was meticulous in dissecting the core elements and articulating in written form the rules of play and game strategies for many card games.

Whist lost its popularity in England for a period. However, the game continued to maintain its popular status in the U.S. The game re-emerged in England with a new name, Bridge. It had new variations, a dummy hand, revised scoring, selection of trump, doubling, etc. The game of Bridge also has a scattered history, and its date of origin varies with different authorities. I found several references to George Washington playing Bridge, so this fact would establish it in America before 1799.[14] The games of Whist and Bridge co-existed in the mid-1800s, although the playing of both games became somewhat dormant. There was a resurgence of both games in the latter part of the century, and the newer game of Bridge supplanted Whist.

Around 1904, Auction Bridge appeared. Every player had a chance to bid for the right to name trumps. Auction Bridge supplanted Bridge and became the new game of choice. Later, around 1925, Contract Bridge developed and became the game of choice. Whist apparently did not regain major prominence until the 1800s, followed by Bridge and Bid Whist in the latter part of the century. Today, people play Whist internationally in a variety of game versions.

[14] http://www.bridgehands.com/H/History_of_Bridge.htm

Is This a Chicken or the Egg Argument?

The logical connection of the dots presents a new twist for consideration! Historians have credited the game of Whist as being the parent of Bid Whist, but my research presents a different view of the game's progression. This viewpoint has some very creditable validity, and I will discuss briefly the reasons for my conclusion.

Most historians agree that Bridge appeared prior to Bid Whist. However, did Bid Whist develop from Whist or was the game a progeny of Bridge? I created some comparisons of the key elements in all three games, and the comparison chart produced this new question about the game's lineage.

Each of the three games is similar in the basic style:

	Whist	*Bridge*	*Bid Whist*
Use of Jokers			X
Use of Bidding process		X	X
Use of No Trump bids		X	X
Use of Downtown bids			X
Use of Kitty			X

However, the game of Whist lacks all the core elements of Bid Whist. The game of Bridge has more overall similarities. This is the basis of why Bridge apparently played a major role or 'the' parenting role of Bid Whist. Bridge had a major influence on the creation of the game of Bid Whist. The comparison chart highlights why White people called the game Black Bridge, and not Black Whist. This theory offers a very plausible explanation to the paradoxical statements about Whist being the father of Bid Whist, and you can make your own judgment, of course.

The comparative information reflects that two of the major elements of Bridge became key components of Bid Whist, and these two "genetic connections" could not possibly have come from the game of Whist. Whist might be the grandfather; however, the game of Bridge would be the father of Bid Whist. The affinity between Bridge and Bid Whist is very clear. In the words of that popular phrase used on the television talk programs, *"Mr. Whist, you are NOT the father!"*

The evidence clearly shows that Whist does have a connectional likeness to both Bridge and Bid Whist. However, the evidence appears to support the fact that Bridge evolved from Whist. Weighing this together within the chronological sequence, it becomes evident that our slave ancestors used cross-breeding to create Bid Whist, a hybrid that captured elements from both Whist and Bridge. The comparison chart of the games gave me a greater appreciation of the ingenuity and creativeness of our ancestors. They created new and challenging features for Bid Whist that far surpassed all the game's predecessors. Thus, we have identified the seed of the game.

CHAPTER TWO

Tracking the Startup-
Fertilization of the Seed

Thus, having established the source of the Bid Whist seed, we can proceed with an investigation of the fertilization step. The investigation of this step in the process presented the greatest challenge because there were no published books on Bid Whist in the 1800s. Whist and Bridge appeared in America, and both games gained popularity. The focus of this book is primarily on Bid Whist, and I will only address the other two games as needed to connect the dots that point to the African American connectional influence. I will occasionally share some significant related facts that provide a better understanding of our African American history or a chronological comparison between the games.

The claims of Bid Whist's origination are undocumented, but historians believe that during the days of slavery, many slaves played Bid Whist on the plantations. Historians have accepted the truth of this theory because of a preponderance of oral interviews and occasional references attesting to these facts. Unfortunately, Bid Whist was not considered to be worthy of written documentation during that period.

It appears that the game played by our slave ancestors would have begun as the game of Whist. Later, the game morphed into Bid Whist. I found evidence that Blacks engaged in Whist and Bid Whist, but there was no evidence in books, newspapers, oral statements, or diaries substantiating Whites playing Bid Whist before 1910. This absence of evidence of Whites playing Bid Whist was the compelling reason that historians connected it to our slave ancestors. Existing information supports this, and I will offer additional corroboration for this theory during a later discussion on the entrance of the Jokers into the game.

Most plantation owners forbade slaves to learn to read and write, for fear that the knowledge would lead to revolts and uprisings.[15] Plantation owners did allow their slaves to play cards. It improved the counting skills needed in their fieldwork to tally bales of cotton, livestock, and other assets. The slaves put their own spin on Whist, and it eventually morphed into the Bid Whist game that lives on today. The chronological order of the available information appears to support the theory generally accepted by historians that Bid Whist originated with Black people who were either slaves or former slaves. There is evidence that some slaves and Free Blacks were playing Whist as early as 1841. The records in scattered diaries and other writings support the theory that slaves originally played the game of Whist, and not Bid Whist as

---

[15] A Virginia law passed in the early 1830s prohibited teaching Blacks to read or write.

we know it today. An excerpt from the diary of Horace C. Lee, a
Freed Black man, reads:

Wednesday Jany 26th 1842

A beautiful spring like morning. Weather much milder than it was yesterday.
Business opened a little better than it has for some time before though it will
not probably last all day. Business not bad all day. In the evening went up to
Mary Peck per invitation & found Persis Mahala Elihu & Mary playing
cards. I looked on a while & then went out to see Mrs. Peck. After talking
awhile with her, I played Whist till 10 & then went home with Persis &
Mahala. Got to bed about 11."[16]

The scarcity of published materials on Bid Whist during the
period from 1865 to 1920 adds fuel to the belief that the game
was indeed an African American creation. When slavery ended
in 1863, most of America was predominately playing the game of
Whist, not the game of Bridge. The Jokers did not appear until
around 1862.[17] Either the slaves did not begin to play Bid Whist
until 1862 or they participated in a hybrid game that encompassed
both Bridge and Whist without the Jokers.

Bridge was not a major influence in the U.S. until the 1800s and
gained prominence after the turn of the century. There are references to Whist in many of the world's most classic novels, such as
The Murders in the Rue Morgue, Around the World in Eighty Days, Gone
With the Wind, Horatio Hornblower, Pride and Prejudice, Groucho and

[16] Farmer, P. G. (n.d.). *The Diary of Horace C. Lee, 1841-1842 (Part2)*.
[17] (A Brief History of Playing Cards, 2007 August) U.S. Playing Card Co.

Me, and DC comic books *Starman*. Many Italian and French novels mentioned Whist.

The evidence indicates that our slave ancestors were playing the game of Whist. At some point after 1862, they combined features from the games of Whist and Bridge, along with the two new Jokers, to create their own game. It is evident that the game of Bridge had an impact on the creation of Bid Whist, as there are many similarities in the two games. Our slave ancestors cloned the name "Bid Whist" because it sounded similar to "Bridge Whist," where the players' bid to gain control during the game. They believed that the term "bid" was a more descriptive adjective than "bridge."

Thus, the game became Bid Whist, and our slave ancestors made all four players active participants for two reasons. The first reason was that none of them wished to sit idly by while the other three played. The second reason might be that no Freed Black at that time would accept the designated Bridge role of "dummy." These factors were among the empirical data that suggests the steps of progression would have been from Whist to Bridge to Bid Whist. All of the above factors undoubtedly contributed to the creation of this new game, called "Black Bridge" by the White community.

The creation of Bid Whist occurred during an era when our African-born ancestors were desperately trying to survive a condition of involuntary servitude in a strange land. The slaves practiced "Waste not, want not" as a daily principle, and their strong survival instinct had taught them to make the best use of every item. Any item found among the trash in the slave quarters was definitely worthless and was far beyond recycling. Our ancestors remained consistent with their principles of making good use of everything, and they created a use for the new Jokers in their card game.

The introduction of the Jokers was a defining moment for the game of Bid Whist. The use of the Jokers as ranking trump cards made Bid Whist a new entity. It gave the game a recognizable difference from the games of Whist and Bridge. The game was unique and called Black Bridge in the White circles!

CHAPTER THREE

The Growth of "Black Bridge"

With the seed planted and fertilized, there was now a brand new card game in the South. The Whist and Bridge players were unimpressed with this fresh game. Whites ridiculed and scorned the game, and named the game Black Bridge. Affluent people used their influence to prevent most printed references to the game in books and newspapers. The White community, until late in the century, used the misnomer Black Bridge. For several years, this hampered the growth of the game outside of certain pockets in the South. However, despite the ridicule from Whist and Bridge players, the recently emancipated slaves continued to play Bid Whist.

I use the term slave, former slave, and slave ancestors rather interchangeably because the evidence strongly supports the game as a Black creation. However, it is unknown whether the game's creator was a slave or a Freed slave. The legal chattel designation of the Bid Whist creators is indeterminable. The 1860 census documents that there were 1.5 million Freed slaves in America.[18] The possibility does exist that a Freed Black created the game.

---

[18] http://www.ushistory.org/us/27d.asp--Many slaves became free through manumission, the voluntary emancipation of a slave by a slave-owner.

The creation of a new card game by slaves/former slaves did not receive recognition or acceptance from the White community. It existed in relative invisibility for years, mainly within the Southern Black community in the South. The game was virtually unknown outside of the South, except in instances where slaves had migrated to other states outside of the Southerly region. Then in 1867, the game received the critical nourishment needed for its survival and growth.

The tracking of Bid Whist's history shows its close relationship with the Emancipation Proclamation and the establishing of the Pullman Palace Car Company in 1867. This linear progression reinforces the belief that Blacks created Bid Whist during the last years of involuntary servitude, and the game was the invention of our slave ancestors.

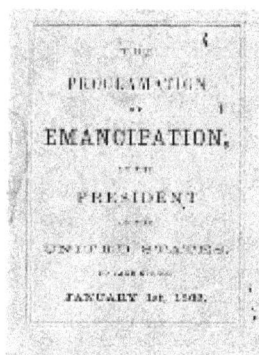

The Pullman Porters - the Ambassadors of Bid Whist

The game of Bid Whist maintained its unheralded existence and popularity in the South. It was like a rare and beautiful flower growing on the top of a mountain with its allure hidden to the rest of the country. Then, in 1867, the Black Pullman porters transplanted the enjoyment of the game to fertile ground in other parts of the country. The evolution of Bid Whist was a direct result of the new work opportunities for Blacks on the railroad. It afforded them inexpensive mobility and access to other states.

The Growth of
"Black Bridge"

The Black community across the country had quickly developed an affinity with the new Pullman porters,[19] who, under the leadership of A. Philip Randolph, organized the Brotherhood of Sleeping Car Porters, the first Black trade union. The Pullman porters were all from the South, and many of them played Bid Whist.

The Pullman porters popularized Bid Whist by introducing the game to other railroad workers and to Black people in other cities. The Pullman porters exported Bid Whist to many areas outside of the South. It was during the Pullman porter era that the term Black Bridge began to fade and the game again acquired its proper name, Bid Whist.

After slavery but before the automotive industry gained prominence, there were few job opportunities for Black men on a large scale. Talented Black men possessing needed skills found jobs, started their own businesses, and began to create their place in society. Some history books have noted the many accomplishments of Black men. However, during that era, few communities were willing to accept more than a few Blacks serving in certain roles. The residents believed that Blacks should not take jobs away from the White majority, unless White men could not perform the tasks.

The emergence of the Pullman Palace Car Company changed the employment opportunities for Black men. George Pullman established the company in 1867. By 1920, the Pullman Company was the leading employer of Blacks. It employed more Af-

---

[19] (Shaw, 1898) Nine Thousand miles on a Pullman Train

rican Americans than any other business in the country.[20] After the death of Mr. Pullman, the leadership of the company passed to Robert Todd Lincoln, the first son of Abraham Lincoln. The porters on the Pullman sleeper cars were among the few African Americans who enjoyed stable employment in the late nineteenth and early twentieth centuries.

The Pullman Company had a need for porters on each of their sleeper cars. These cars offered sleeping and dining accommodations to elite White passengers traveling on long trips across the country. The jobs were stable, and although the pay was not great, the porters received added income from tips from passengers. Their income (with tips) was considerably higher than that of available jobs during that era. The porters were intelligent young men who tactfully catered to the wishes of the passengers to generate high tips, but in such a way that built the job into a profession. These talented men made a good living by providing excellent service while avoiding the pitfall of allowing their job to be viewed as a "lackey position."

This large influx of new jobs for the ex-slaves was the first step in the evolution of Bid Whist. The porters were the catalyst that propelled the game from isolated pockets in the South to other parts of the country. The original Pullman porters were former slaves who lived in the southern areas where Bid Whist originated. Not all the Pullman porters played Bid Whist; however, the porters familiar with the game introduced Bid Whist to their fellow

---

[20] (The Legacy of Pullman Porters, n.d.)

workers and their newly established friends during their long trips across the country.

These men, some of whom were college graduates, were highly respected in the Black community. Many notable African Americans worked as Pullman porters.

• Benjamin Mays, former president of Morehouse College

• Matthew Henson, first African American to explore the Arctic•

• Gordon Parks, award-winning photojournalist and director of the *Shaft* and *Learning Tree* movies

• Nat Love[21] (shown in photo on right, also known as Deadwood Dick), a legendary cowboy and frontiersman who later joined the ranks of the porters

In My Fighting Clothes

• Edward Nixon, civil rights activist and one of the organizers of the Montgomery bus boycott

• Big Bill Broonzy, renowned blues musician inducted into the Blues Hall of Fame

With the meals served and the passengers settled into their sleeping quarters, the porters could enjoy a moment of rest and relaxation. The porters found that playing Bid Whist was a welcome and relaxing part of their day. They also played Bid Whist during their runs. The game was fun and helped pass the time as the train rolled from town to town across the country. The Pullman por-

---

[21] http://en.wikipedia.org/wiki/Nat_Love

ters tweaked and refined the game to be equal to the challenge of the "thinking man." More porters became familiar with the game, and they began to play at different homes, boarding houses,[22] and nightclubs during trip layovers.

The porters enjoyed the jovial moments of trash talking, as it offered a sort of pressure release valve for the tremendous daily stress that came with being a Black man in that era. The trash talking became a major part of Bid Whist. The humor elevated the porters' enjoyment of the game and is still one of the most enjoyed features of the game today.

How did the Lingo and Trash-Talking Begin?

The Library of Congress has among its artifacts several audio interviews with former Pullman porters conducted by earlier authors. Many of those interviews contain warm memories of the Pullman porters' endearment to the game of Bid Whist. They created a card game that allowed them to display their wit and adaptability to challenge. They created their own lingo and a form of trash talkin',[23] which afforded them many laughable moments during the games, and both became lasting and endearing parts of playing Bid Whist.

Most people mistakenly equate the lingo and trash talking as the same thing, but they are not. Trash talking in the servitude era was an outlet for the stress encountered daily by the slaves. During

---

[22] Myers, R. a. (2005). *Remembering the Path to T-Town: Migration of an African American Family through Seven States to Lincoln, Nebraska*. Washington, DC:

[23] Originally an abbreviated slang term for "trash talking"

that era, it was dangerous for a Black person to talk back to a White person. During their Bid Whist games, the slaves could privately talk to each other and jovially blurt out comical retorts they would have said to Whites if not for fear of severe punishment. They all understood that silence was their key to survival. However, in the secrecy and safety of their private game, they could be boisterous and act out humorous responses directed only at each other.

The trash-talking moments allowed the slaves to display their intelligence and quick wit, which stayed hidden while doing their daily chores. The modern phrase "Bragging Rights" is an offshoot slang of trash talking. Recently, a Chicago popular female comedian shared her opinion that trash talking was one of the earliest forms of "Improv" comedy, which set the stage for the many Celebrity Roasts that have aired on American television. The Pullman porters continued this practice in their new jobs and exhibited their quick wit and flair for improvisation. They shared this exciting brand new game with people during their days off and layovers.

Trash talking was an original part of the game from slavery days, but their new employment as Pullman porters introduced the former slaves to a new job-related language. The porters began to incorporate terms from the recently learned railroad lingo to describe Bid Whist game maneuvers. They created terminology coined from the words used daily in their work. For example, a cross-country run from a major western hub to Boston was "going all the way." Thus, if a team won all the books in a hand, it was "running a Boston."[24]

There was another significance in using the term "Boston." The city was a major transportation hub as it provided convergence points for the trains and the shipping docks. This transportation hub status of the City of Boston understandably made it the end of the line stop for many cross-country train lines. Even more significant was the fact that the City of Boston was the personification of freedom for most Black people during the late 1800s.

During the period of the Civil War, Boston was a city that represented the ideas and principles of human freedom. The Boston school system integrated in the late 1800s, and generally, there was progressive thinking within the Bostonian community. During the Civil War, the Union Army recruited Blacks from across the country to join the Army's Black Regiment, the 54th Massachusetts Regiment. There were thousands of Black men "trying to get to Boston" to enlist in the Union Army and enjoy the personal freedom and liberty offered by that community.

---

[24] Illustration used with permission of CafePress Inc. 1850 Gateway Drive, Suite 300, San Mateo, CA 94404. Further reproduction prohibited.

The Growth of
"Black Bridge"

Bid Whist allows a player to indicate whether the ranking sequence of the cards will be a high cards win (going Uptown) or low cards win (going Downtown). The porters used this as a reference to the geographical layout of most eastern cities, and it denoted that a Freed Black could choose to go to either part of the city.

Incidentally, we should mention that Pullman in 1880 built a company town (now a historic landmark called the Pullman District) on the Southside of Chicago, which was a model town. The Pullman District was an area where you could always find a good Bid Whist game. In 1880, the Pullman area had one of the highest Black populations in the country. However, it was not a Black town by any means. The residents were predominately White, and they enjoyed a very good life with all the amenities. The Pullman community had a big fancy hotel, company stores, luxurious homes, and tenement homes. The tenement homes offered decent housing for the Black residents, which was better than other surrounding parts of the city. The community later annexed to the City of Chicago.

Not every Pullman porter played cards, and I was unable to identify those individual porters who introduced the game to the aggregate group. The Great Chicago Fire of 1871 destroyed the

Photo: Off-duty porters playing Whist (Library of Congress)

company employee records on the original Pullman porters. This group must share the credit collectively as the founding ambassadors of Bid Whist.

The name of the first Pullman porter is unknown. However, during my research, I did find one humorous anecdote that exhibits the wit of the Pullman porter:

A traveler informed a Pullman agent that he wanted a Pullman berth. "Upper or lower," asked the agent. "What's the difference?" he asked. "A difference of fifty cents," replied the agent. "The lower is higher than the upper. The higher price is for the lower. If you want it lower, you'll have to go higher. We sell the upper lower than the lower. In other words, the higher the lower. Most people don't like the upper, although it is lower on account of it's being higher. When you occupy an upper, you have to get up to go to bed and get down to get up. You can have the lower if you pay higher. The upper is lower than the lower because it is higher. If you are willing to go higher, it will be lower." But the poor man had fainted.[25]

Though not well known, it is of significant historical importance that the Pullman porters helped to establish the *Chicago Defender* newspaper's rise to the first Black publication to have over one hundred thousand readers. The Pullman porters also helped increase the distribution of the *Pittsburgh Courier*. The porters accomplished this by distributing copies of the papers to Black residents living along the routes of their trains through the South. The newspapers distributed by the porters became the only source of reliable information for many Black people in the South.

---

[25] Source: Southern California Scenic Railway Library

The Pullman porters left many great legacies to the Black communities. They very gracefully struggled with the racial issues of their times while building an outstanding record of service and much-deserved respect. They laid the foundation for modern civil rights actions and union membership for African Americans, and they blazed the path for today's generations. Their story is extraordinary, and there are many books about their many accomplishments.[26]

The ten thousand men who served as Pullman porters were the first and the most significant step in the game's evolution. The porters became the vanguard for Bid Whist. The Pullman porters provided national exposure for Bid Whist. The second step in the growth period was very powerful because of the enormous magnitude of players involved in its spread across the country. This important next step was the result of the migration patterns of Black people after 1910, which propelled the popularity of Bid Whist to a much higher level.

The Great Migrations were Major Influences upon Bid Whist

The first Great Migration around 1910 produced a huge surge in the popularity of Bid Whist. Two million Blacks moved to the North, West, and Midwest, bringing with them many of their southern traditions, including Soul Food cooking and Bid Whist. The second Great Migration occurred from 1920-1940.

---

[26] (The Legacy of Pullman Porters, n.d.) Retrieved from http://www.museumoftheamericanrailroad.org/Resources/

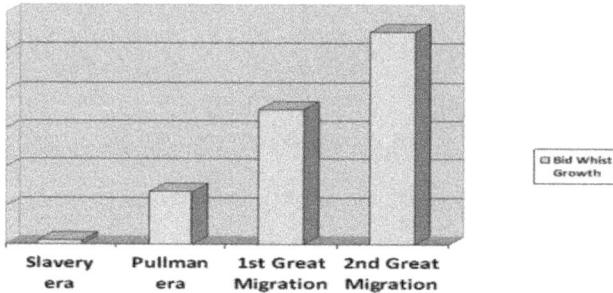

Bid Whist Growth

Slavery era | Pullman era | 1st Great Migration | 2nd Great Migration

Another five million Blacks left the South, bringing even more Bid Whist players to other parts of the country.[27]   During the 1920s, my hometown Chicago alone grew to a population of more than a million African Americans. Many people believe Bid Whist started around 1920. This was only a misconception created by the relatively sudden appearance of several million new Bid Whist players in the North.

Black College Students Played a Major Role

There was another major element in the growth of Bid Whist that continues even today. Most books have not recognized the impact of the Black college students who played the game on campus. The third factor in the game's evolution was the influence of those Black college students who went away to study at higher learning institutions and introduced Bid Whist to their fellow students. The image of the game was elevated as professional people began to play Bid Whist.

---

[27] http://blackhistory.com/content/64166/the-great-migration

The Growth of "Black Bridge"

Many colleges and universities established across the country during the late 1800s were open to Black student enrollment, and many of the Black students played Bid Whist. However, the main thrust of the game's growth was within the vertices of a triangle formed by the cities of Chicago, IL; Atlanta, GA; and Ithaca, NY. These college cities also had a large number of residents who were Pullman porters, and they stimulated play of the game within their home areas.

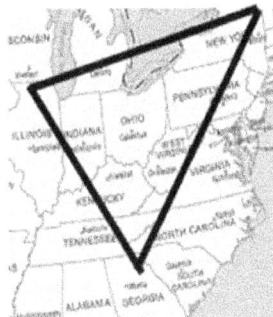

Former college students frequently reminisce about their fond memories of a classic Bid Whist game that occurred during their under-graduate studies. One such story about the relationship-building power of Bid Whist came from the Library of Congress. During an interview with William Beverly Carter Jr., (America's first African American Ambassador-at-Large), Mr. Carter warmly discussed his college days at Lincoln University and his first experiences at playing Bid Whist with his classmates.[28]

Many Black students used the game of Bid Whist as a bridge to connect with other students and to build new relationships. Some of the students became so smitten with the game that you had to 'beat them with a stick' to make them go to class.

Bid Whist became an unofficial college elective subject, and the game was a "rite-of-passage" among Black college students. Most college campuses across the country had some form of Bid

---

[28] http://hdl.loc.gov/loc.mss/mfdip.2010car01 - Interview with Ambassador William Beverly Carter Jr.

Whist parties. Mostly, college Bid Whist parties were informal gatherings, but many liberal colleges formally sanctioned and supported these events. Included in this category of Bid Whist college students are the fraternity brothers and sorority sisters of our Black Greek organizations, which often hosted Bid Whist events.

Earlier, I mentioned the intelligence of the Pullman porters. There is evidence that some of them matriculated at the new universities established after 1860. Documents at the Cornell University Library reflect evidence of the Black Student Union group that hosted many Bid Whist tournaments throughout its history. A group established the American Whist Congress in Ithaca, NY around 1886, again reflecting the fact that the surrounding area shared a strong interest in the game.

Thus, the Pullman porters, the two Great Migrations, and the Black college students were significant factors contributing to the growth of Bid Whist.

CHAPTER FOUR

The Establishment of Bid Whist in America

By 1940, the Bid Whist seed grew into a large tree with branches across the United States. This leads to a discussion on expansion because with growth comes the necessity for sustainability. In America, the game became a strong part of African American cultural heritage past, present, and future. The game of Bid Whist found wide acceptance in most Black communities across the nation, and it is now enjoyed by multiple generations of Blacks, having been passed down for four and five generations dating back to before the Civil War.

Bid Whist has become a popular and quite enjoyable African American past-time. The game has increased in popularity because it is a very engaging and fun hobby. Bid Whist's popularity no doubt increased in the Black community because the playing of card games was a very inexpensive form of recreation. The only required equipment is a deck of playing cards. This simple and singular requirement is no doubt why our slave ancestors quickly embraced the game, because all they needed was a scrapped deck of cards from the slave-owner's trash. I have conjured up visions in my mind of our slave ancestors surviving by scavenging for discarded food scraps, but I never thought about other throwaways that would be useful to an indentured slave. It is ironic that some of those items led to the creation of Soul Food cooking, Bid Whist, quilt making,[29] and other enduring traditions in the Black community.

Today, over seventy percent of the Black community has played Bid Whist, and overall, ninety-five percent of African Americans are aware of the game. Currently, there are Bid Whist clubs in most of our major cities, and the members of these clubs host their own tournaments for prizes and bragging rights.[30] There are several sites on the web where people play live against other players across the country, and there are Bid Whist telephone apps available for smart-phones.[31]

The game of Bid Whist continues to grow and flourish as a favorite card game, particularly among African Americans. Friends meet and play regularly. Bid Whist groups and social clubs have formed in cities and towns across the country. The Bid Whist and social clubs became people-gathering events that supported the continuation of the game's rich heritage and its growth in popularity as the game passed from generation to generation. This group of

---

[29] During the American Civil War, slaves used quilts as a means to share and transmit secret messages to escape slavery and travel the Underground Railroad. http://www.owensound.ca/live/underground-railroad

[30] (Card Sharks Inc.) (National Bid Whist Association, n.d.) (Midwest Bid Whist Association)

[31] (www.whistportal.com, n.d.) (Case's Online, n.d.)

avid Bid Whist players sustained the continued expansion of Bid Whist into the twenty-first century.

A newspaper columnist, Darryl Owens, wrote very eloquently the following short article captured in print by some newspapers:

"Just as blacks living under segregation found comfort Sundays in church, many others found community Saturday nights in an orphaned card game that they made their own.

Bid whist, or "Bid" as it is known by the faithful, is a variant of whist, a card game born in England that became popular with the powdered-wig set in Europe and America in the 1800s. Near the turn of the century, whist gave rise to bridge, and whites abandoned whist for its offspring, which they considered more intellectual.

Whist went underground, where black servants adopted it, embraced it, adapted it. Over time the game, popular with Pullman porters on cross-country trips, spread, evolved and absorbed an African American aesthetic.

For blacks living "free" but still segregated, bid whist offered freedom to shake off the repression, to let loose. To shout. To thunk down cards on the table when winning a trick. Cards became a sporting event.

It was brassy. It was community. It was theirs."[32]

The Civil Rights Movement of the 1960s marked another surge in the playing of Bid Whist, as many Bid Whist parties doubled as

---

[32] (Darryl C. Owens, 2004) The Orlando Sentinel; Knight Ridder/Tribune News Service

civil rights meetings. The popularity of Bid Whist continued to increase in the ensuing years, and the last decade has been no exception. Today, people play the game in almost every state in the union, and in England, France, Norway, Sweden, Switzerland, Belgium, many other nations, and even the continent of Antarctica.

There was a syndicated television program, *Bid Whist Party Throwdown*, which featured well-known actors and entertainers competing at Bid Whist for charity. This show was highly entertaining as the celebrities slapped the cards on the table or slapped the winning card on their forehead, and engaged in some jovial trash talking.

The significant rise in the playing of the game was the direct result of the Black Student Unions on many college campuses. The growing number of regional Bid Whist associations and social clubs, and the increasing play at local taverns, the online websites, and the many new mobile apps, were also contributing factors in the growth of Bid Whist.

The local newspapers in some cities have been amazed at the new-found acceptance of the game, and they have frequently sent reporters to interview the patrons and to report on the phenomenal new interest in the game. The game became so popular that a major daily paper included a column on Bid Whist. In the 1990s, Ms. Angel Beck had the only syndicated column on Bid Whist in the nation.

The growing number of Bid Whist social clubs perpetuates the popularity of Bid Whist across the country. Bid Whist originated in the South, but today the game exists in almost every state.

The National Card Sharks Inc. and the National
Bid Whist Association are the two largest Bid
Whist associations in the country. These associations have established multiple chapters across
the United States, and they annually host several
tournaments in different cities with food, entertainment, and the awarding of impressively large
trophies and medals to the winners.[33]

The new local associations and social clubs across the country host regularly scheduled events in their areas. Some of them
provide daily playing hours in their clubhouses or donated space
at event halls. The Robinson Barbeque Sauce Company (a nationally known product in supermarkets) opened the hall next to their
restaurant to host Bid Whist events. Similarly, many neighborhood taverns have seen major increases in their profits because of
the many new patrons that visit their establishments on Bid Whist
nights.

The Afrocentric nature of Bid Whist also created a growth in
the playing of other card games (Spades, Hearts, Tonk, and Coon-
can) across the country. The U.S. Games Systems Inc. in 1977
produced a custom "Black History Playing Card Deck." Each of
the individual playing cards illustrated a famous African American,
including Duke Ellington, Dr. Martin Luther King Jr., Jesse Owens, Bill Pickett, Harriett Tubman, Sojourner Truth, Malcolm X,

---

[33] (National Card Sharks, n.d.) (National Bid Whist Association, n.d.)

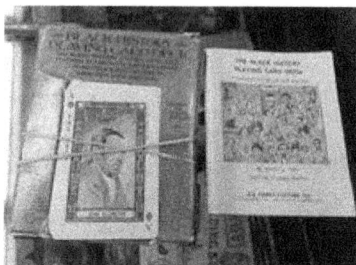

Jackie Robinson and other notables. The box of cards included a booklet containing the biographies of each of the individuals.[34]

Many nonprofit organizations have begun to hold annual tournaments as fundraising events for their groups. Hundreds of organizations have incorporated Bid Whist events in their annual conferences, scholarship fundraisers, and general fundraising initiatives. A new trend, which recently began in Georgia, is the hosting of weekly Bid Whist gatherings by Baptist churches. The members of the Congressional Black Caucus host annual Bid Whist tournaments. The Miller Beer Co.,[35] the National Association of Black Journalists, and the NAACP[36] have presented other tournaments. During the 2012 presidential election campaign, Bid Whist parties were fundraising events for President Obama. The inclusion of Bid Whist activities was a very effective method to gain increased attendance at events.[37]

My research produced a long list of celebrities, athletes, politi-

---

[34] Illustrations from the Black History Playing Card Deck used with permission of U.S. Games Systems, Inc., Stamford, CT 06902. c. 1977 by U.S. Games Systems, Inc. Further reproduction prohibited.

[35] Sweatshirts awarded (see page 53) to regional finalists in the Miller Beer Co. national Bid Whist Tournament, 1988

[36] Black Enterprise, Nov. 1999

[37] http://www.nytimes.com/1997/03/09/nyregion/a-new-bid-for-bid-whist.html

cal leaders, and other well-known people who have a fond affection for Bid Whist. There have been many Bid Whist players in the U.S. House of Representatives, but Carol Mosely Braun (the first and only African American woman elected to the U.S. Senate) was the first person to introduce Bid Whist to the Senate.[38] A Washington Post article alluded to President Barack Obama playing Bid Whist while vacationing in Hawaii,[39] and there was an article on BlackAmericaWeb.com that also referenced the subject.[40] Mr. Obama did mention in his book, *Dreams of My Father*, about his observing an outdoor Bid Whist game, and it is quite possible that during the days that our 44th U.S. President lived on the

Southside of Chicago, he learned to play Bid Whist. We mentioned previously about the annual Bid Whist tournament hosted by the Congressional Black Caucus; there are too many federal, state, and city officials who play Bid Whist to name them all.

Michael Jordan and Wilt Chamberlain are included in the list of great athletes recognized as excellent Bid Whist players. The legendary blues musician, Buddy Guy, received mention as a good Bid Whist player.[41] Terry Saban, the wife of Alabama's head football coach Nick Saban, learned to play Bid Whist so that she could

---

[38] http://www.chicagoreader.com/chicago/old-hands/
Content?oid=898162

[39] Rucker, Philip Washington Post Staff Writer, Friday, December 26, 2008

[40] http://blackamericaweb.com/2014/06/23/welcome-back-to-bid-whist/

[41] http://www.livebluesworld.com/profiles/blog/show?id=1598513%3ABlogPost%3A259

play the game with recruits.[42] Countless other people should be on this list, but there are not enough pages in this book.

The last ten years have witnessed another tremendous upsurge in the international popularity of this game. Although the game of Whist originated in Europe, its hybrid form Bid Whist began in America. Bid Whist and Poker are among the few card games that are products of the United States. Bid Whist was played primarily in the U.S. and for many years remained relatively unknown (with some exceptions) among European Americans. However, the popularity of online games has created a new enthusiasm for the game abroad.[43] The popularity of Bid Whist overseas is the result of the increased international communications created by the ever-growing usage of the Internet, which allows people to play Bid Whist with other people living thousands of miles away.

[42] http://bamasocialnetwork.com/terry-saban-nicks-wifalabama-fans-appreciative-leaving/
[43] (Case's Online, n.d.)

CHAPTER FIVE
Bid Whist's Period of Expansion and Maturity

A lthough these are separate steps in the evolution process, I have combined them because the status of Bid Whist falls indistinguishably between the two levels. The game currently is in a renewed expansion level because of the new online games. Case's Ladder Online claims to have over thirteen million members.[44] Not all of them are Bid Whist players; nevertheless, it is an unbelievable number of online players. Bid Whist's amazing longevity places it contiguously at the maturity level.

Numerous notable Whist clubs around the country have been in existence for many, many years. There were countless Whist clubs in the late nineteenth century. Among the most notable of the Whist clubs were the Southern Whist Club at 261 Wabash, Chicago, IL; The Whist Club at 6 E. 61st, New York, NY; and the University and Whist Club at 805 N. Broom, Wilmington, DE.

Although, not established until after the turn of the century, one of the oldest African American Whist clubs still in existence is the Owls Whist Club. The club was founded on February 14, 1914, in Charleston, South Carolina, by twelve young men who wanted to get together just to have

---

[44] (Case's Online, n.d.)

fun.[45] All of the men were active in their respective professions and the community. They wanted to find some time and a place just to play cards and discuss the things that affected the lives of Black people in Charleston, South Carolina and the nation at the turn of the twentieth century. On February 14, 2014, the club celebrated its one-hundredth anniversary.

Bid Whist and the Law

Added emphasis on the popularity of Bid Whist and its recognition in the United States became evident with the game of Bid Whist being the subject matter of an article published in the *California Law Review* in 1993.[46] I was quite surprised to find a reference to Bid Whist in one of the leading law journals. The article discussed the negative impact that two major Supreme Court decisions had on our nation's Black Colleges and upon integration based upon a true freedom of choice. Using the games of Tonk and Bid Whist, the author illustrated the erroneous and flawed findings in *The United States vs. Fordice* and *Brown vs. the Board of Education* by making the argument that "… the world is richer and improved for both African Americans and Whites when society allows African Americans to choose when they wish to leave the world of Tonk and Bid Whist for the world of Poker and Bridge."

The Bid Whist Seed Continues to Flourish

The Bid Whist seed has grown into a tree that is now at least 150 years old and still growing. Personally, I gained a greater ap-

---

[45] http://owlswhistclub.org/

[46] (Johnson Jr., 1993)Bid Whist, Tonk, and United States v. Fordice: Why Integrationism Fails African Americans Again California Law Review Vol. 81> Iss. 6 (1993)

preciation for the long history of Bid Whist when I visualized this game as a soaring oak tree. The seed planted at the end of slavery has grown through seven generations of African Americans and today stands as a truly magnificent and majestic sight. Its many towering branches stand taller than a seven-story building, and its trunk circumference is wider than the outreach of four adults with joined hands.

The photo on the right is an oak tree in South Carolina around the same age. What a marvelous spot for a Bid Whist Picnic and Celebration!

I have shared with you my collection of facts and other items of interest about the history of Bid Whist developed during my research. Our process outline identifies the last step as the exit stage. Bid Whist shows no signs of declining interest, as displayed in the chart below.

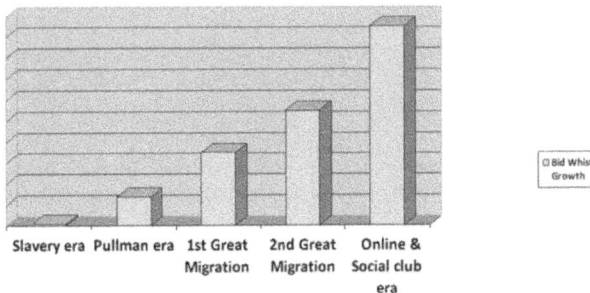

Slavery era Pullman era 1st Great Migration 2nd Great Migration Online & Social club era

☐ Bid Whist Growth

The recent increased international play supported by the worldwide web of computers should sustain the game for many more years.

CHAPTER SIX
Bid Whist -Today and Beyond!

The demise of Bid Whist is certainly not imminent in the near future. Therefore, we can turn our attention to the game of Bid Whist in the twenty-first century and beyond. I hope that your newly accumulated knowledge of the history of Bid Whist will support an informed discussion on the evolution of the game to its present status.

If you have played Bid Whist in different parts of the country, then I am sure you have been amazed at the multitude of variations of Bid Whist played in different states. In large cities, you can often find the game varies in different parts of that city. The differences in playing styles indicate the specific regions where these players first learned to play Bid Whist. If you originally honed your skills in the East, Midwest, or the South, it reflects in your playing style and bidding mannerisms.

The games of Whist and Bridge used the term "hotel rules" to define variations made to the game for shorter or longer play necessitated by the location of the game.[47] Blacks did not usually have access to hotels, and played their Bid Whist games in homes, so this term changed to "house rules." Like any sports activities, game variations occur in unique situations, and players should inquire about the house rules before beginning the game. Most of

---

[47] http://en.wikipedia.org/wiki/Whist

the house rules across the country keep the game organized and standardized according to the customs of that region. Many of the newer rules are house rules that may either reflect the inexperience of the players or are used by more seasoned players to provide an easy and quick-moving game. It is my sincere hope that this book will encourage both new and experienced players to become uniform in their game play, and begin the initiation of standardized play across the country.

Most Bid Whist players either have forgotten or were never aware that the game of Bid Whist was a hybrid offspring of Bridge and Whist, and the game's original rules were combined rules of Whist and Bridge. There has never been any published document creating a nationally recognized and standardized set of rules for Bid Whist players.

Most of the Bid Whist associations and clubs have respectively adopted a set of rules used for participation in tournament level competition. The National Bid Whist Association and Card Sharks Inc. have drafted their own set of rules. They administer these rules during their hosted tournaments.[48] The rules drafted by both groups are comprehensive and effective for tournament settings. However, many players fail to realize that such rules are for use in the hosted tournament, and tournament rules vary within different organizations.

Author Edmond Hoyle has been very limited in his discussion on this game. I have heard many people say that the Book of Hoyle makes this or that statement on the rules of Bid Whist,

---

[48] (Card Sharks, Inc.) http://cardsharksinc.com/index.html

but in most cases, these statements are undocumented and exaggerated. If you read the books by Hoyle, you will only find a few pages on Bid Whist.[49] Most players across the country play the game utilizing regional house rules, which can vary greatly in different parts of the country.

Although some believe Mr. Hoyle was not an expert card player, he earned a very impressive reputation as a person who provided consistently accurate records of game rules. His writings preserved the integrity of most card games and, in so doing, supported the continued growth of many card games. Bid Whist has received little recognition because of its cultural Afrocentric flavor, so it is my sincere hope that this book will establish a degree of uniformity across the nation about the basic rules. Bid Whist will be better served if the national organizations agree upon one universal standard for rules that can be sanctioned by all of their chapters.

I hope that the information presented in this book will enable players to understand that in actual live play (without the safety net of computer software) they will encounter such instances. The computer software used in online games prevents human errors such as reneges and playing out of turn. In actual competition, these violations do occur, and players who originally learned Bid Whist online need to understand the penalties and remedies for such occurrences.

This book should provide many of the answers needed for

---

[49] (Albert Morehead, 1964) (Hoyle, 1743)

actual competition. If a situation should occur that is not covered, the bibliography and glossary of this book offer resources for research and review.

CHAPTER SEVEN
Myths and Mistaken Beliefs about Bid Whist!

The history of Bid Whist spans many years, and there are connectional dots that are still undiscovered. The highlights of the history of Bid Whist have presented some interesting facts about its cultural background and its evolution. At this point, you know more about the history of the game than most of the current players. Before moving to the next section, I should address some myths that cloud the overall history of Bid Whist.

Myth—There are statements that appear on the Internet identifying two separate people as the creator of Bid Whist or the person who introduced the game into America. My research offers documentation to discredit both claims, and I do not believe that either of these men can make such assertions. These two claims created major and serious doubts for me, and although I searched many documents, I found nothing that even remotely validated such claims.

The first claim I found was about a person identified as Mr. Dickerson. That website's information was the only reference that I could find on this person. I could not find his name associated with Bridge, Whist, or Bid Whist on any other websites or any printed materials; nor could I pull up his name on any search engines. I believe someone misinterpreted Internet information and shared Mr. Dickerson's name very innocently. However, many people who read the statement unswervingly believe that he invented the Bid Whist card game.

The second claim on the Internet relating to the creator of Bid Whist struck a bad chord with me.[50] The highly questionable statement appeared on the website of a major playing card manufacturer and credited a European American with the creation of Bid Whist.

This playing card company alleged that the inventor of Bid Whist was a Mr. Phillips, who was the author of many books on Bridge. My research developed several rebuttals. It is strange that Mr. Phillips never published a book on Bid Whist. One would normally expect the creator of the game to share their expertise and insight in a published article. Furthermore, Mr. Phillips was born around 1890, and this was several years after Bid Whist's appearance in America. Mr. Phillips was born and raised in England, with no record of having spent any prolonged time in America. There are no writings on Bid Whist by Mr. Phillips in the catalogue of the Library of London, nor was there any documentation of Bid Whist games in England prior to World War II. Nevertheless, we are to believe that this man invented Bid Whist and then somehow exported the game to America without ever having first established its popularity in England. I reported to the card manufacturer my findings about their statements, and they removed the information without protest.

---

[50] A very humorous television ad aired in 2014 with a rather subliminal message: Do not believe everything you see or hear on the Internet!

Myths and Mistaken Beliefs
about Bid Whist

Many people have already viewed this information, but because they have never seen any retractions, many continue to believe the information. If we use a logical assumption that Bid Whist's creator would have been at least twelve-to-sixteen years of age when they created the game, then the creator/creators of Bid Whist would have been born prior to 1855, to fit the pattern of the game's evolution. This profile would eliminate both Mr. Dickerson and Mr. Phillips as the creator of Bid Whist. There are no printed records to substantiate the names of the game's founder(s). This lack of documentation makes it almost impossible to identify the creator of Bid Whist, but there is ample printed material to refute any inappropriate and unjustifiable claims.

My research suggests that the inventor of Bid Whist would have been living in America around 1862, and would have been a slave or former slave. There is strong evidence suggesting this person would have lived in either Georgia or North Carolina during this time. These two states were the Pullman Company's major recruiting areas in their search for the men originally hired as Pullman porters. When I began my research, the oldest living Pullman porter was 107 years old, and none of the distinguished people interviewed could provide the name of the game's originators. "The conclusion is there is no conclusion." —Daniel Webster

<u>Myth</u>—There is a prevailing myth that Bid Whist began between 1920 and 1940, and others believe Black soldiers brought the game home from overseas. These statements are untrue, and earlier I presented evidence to support this. The second Great

Migration created this misconception. The evidence confirms Bid Whist's presence in the North and South long before 1920.[51] There are Black centenarians and supercentenarians who retold stories of Bid Whist games in the late 1800s. In 2014, the oldest living person in the United States is Jerlean Tally. Ms. Tally is 115 years old and was born in Georgia. She and others are examples of our people resources, containing knowledge and memories about our lineal history.[52] My grandparents (both born in 1898, but now deceased) talked about watching grown-ups play Bid Whist when they were young. These treasured seniors are record-keepers of our heritage, and those still living and of full mental capacity represent an invaluable treasure of information.

Sometimes, published information on Bid Whist was unavailable or inadequate. I focused my research on information found in passages in unrelated book materials and personal diaries. I used the narrations of great-grandparents as corroborative evidence. A passage in one written work spoke of a young Black woman learning the game. She watched the Pullman porters who lived in the same boarding house as her family.[53] There are published articles documenting that Pullman porters played Bid Whist during the late 1800s and early 1900s.[54] There are many excerpts to document the playing of Bid Whist before the twentieth century.

---

[51] http://www.penobscot-maine.com/1920.html
[52] (Current Validated Living Supercentenarians, 2014)
[53] (Myers, Roy and Stephanie, 2005) *Remembering the Path to T-Town*
[54] (Tye, Larry, 2007) *Rising from the Rails, Pullman Porters and the Making of the Black Middle Class*

~~

<u>Myth</u>—A continually-perpetuated myth during the years oc-
curs when supposedly experienced players refer to Hoyle on the
subject of Bid Whist. Mr. Hoyle is a respected authority on many
card games; however, he cannot be a putative authority on the
game of Bid Whist. Mr. Hoyle died in 1769, a century before the
game's invention. If he had lived, I believe Mr. Hoyle would have
captured the game in his usual style of very organized, detailed,
and authoritative writings. Therefore, it is an untruth when players
attempt to validate a questionable Bid Whist issue by stating, "according to Hoyle, this is true in Bid Whist."

<u>Myth</u>—The White Union soldiers taught the game to the
Black soldiers during the Civil War. This is highly unlikely because
both the Union Army and the Confederate Army practiced segregation. Most of the 186,000 enlisted Black soldiers served in the
segregated United States Colored Troop units. The few Blacks
assigned to White units in the Union Army served as assistants to
the cooks. The Black and White soldiers did not fight side by side,
nor did they sleep and eat together. Fraternization between the
races was discouraged in both armies. The White Union soldiers
did not wish to establish any relationships with the Black enlisted
men. The Constitutional Rights Foundation made this comment
on their website: "… inequalities plagued black troops… black
troops remained in segregated units throughout the Civil War."[55]

---

[55] http://www.crf-usa.org/black-history-month/black-troops-in-union-
blue

The books published about Blacks in the Civil War and the writings on the Tuskegee aviators remind us of the great difficulty Blacks encountered in the military before 1949.

There were many diaries written by White and Black Union soldiers that speak of the challenges faced by Black soldiers during the Civil War.[56] One of the diaries did state that Black soldiers received orders to remain in confined areas within their encampments. There was no mention in any of the soldiers' diaries (Black or White) of interracial activities taking place. This state of separatism between the Colored Troop regiments and the White regiments makes it difficult to imagine the prolonged interracial gathering necessary to allow the White Union soldiers to teach the game to Black soldiers.

A few of the diaries mention that the White soldiers played Euchre (the first known game to use Jokers), and the diaries of the Black soldiers comment on the game of Whist being played by the Colored Troops. Bid Whist was a relatively obscure game played in the South and only by the Southern Blacks. Southern Whites scorned the game, and it is very unlikely that Northern Whites were aware of the game. There is no evidence that any Whites played Bid Whist during that era, especially in the North. All of the facts suggest there is no validity to the statement that White soldiers taught the game during the Civil War.

Myth—I have witnessed players exhibiting frustrations when their partner took out an opponent's bid when their teammate had

[56] (Massachusetts Historical Society, n.d.) http://www.masshist.org/collection-guides/view/fa0244

no hand. They sometimes tell their partner that a pass would have been a better choice, and they state, "Pass is a bid!"

For the record, Pass is not a bid! This statement is a common misnomer, as the history of the game clearly shows that Pass is an available option, not a bid. Each player has two options; the player can either Bid or Pass. This fact is in the older rulebooks from Bridge and Whist. If you have played the game for a while, you probably have heard the statement "Bid or Pass." That statement is evidence that a player has these options. The player makes either a bid or options to pass.

When a player chooses to indicate the strength of his hand, the player makes a bid. If a player chooses not to indicate their hand strength (perhaps the player has no significant cards), then the player may exercise his other option and elect to pass. The rules of Bid Whist require at least one bid be made on each deal. This rule would be unnecessary if a Pass is a bid.

There are other myths created by the new variations of the game. It was the myths, the undocumented statements, and other incorrect inferences that provided the motivation for writing this book. I wanted to capture the core elements and history of Bid Whist in a structured format, which effectively presented the documented facts from either oral testimony or substantiated written materials.

SECTION II

Rules and Game Strategies

CHAPTER EIGHT
A Review of the Game's Components

The historical review of Bid Whist revealed that the game was a combined version of Whist and Bridge. Well, Bid Whist itself has morphed into several popular forms of the game. More than ten distinctive card games fall within the Bid Whist family. In this section, I will focus on the different versions of the game, the game rules, and game strategies.

I should first discuss the Kitty and the Jokers because most of our later discussions will frequently mention these two terms. The use of the Jokers and the Kitty in the game of Bid Whist are the elements that make the game unique.

The Kitty

An important part of most versions of Bid Whist is the Kitty, and many players place a lot of emphasis on the Kitty. Originally, Bid Whist players used a six-card Kitty, but today the game's evolution has produced many different versions in the Kitty's structure. Some of the versions use no Kitty, but most versions incorporate the use of a Kitty that contains four to six cards. The Kitty is a <u>bonus of extra cards</u> awarded to the player who wins the bidding process on the deal. No one is sure where this term originated. There is a card game called Kitty that is not similar to Bid Whist. However, some believe the term was a carryover from one of the other card games. The word could have come into use two ways. The word may have come from 'kit', a collection of supplies. It could also be from 'Kitty', a term used to describe a prison or lock-up. Both explanations have validity in that the Kitty does become a supply kit for the victorious bidder. Furthermore, the Kitty remains locked to all players and the key to unlocking the Kitty belongs to the winning bidder.[57]

Some regions require the winning bidder to place the Kitty on the table face up, and expose the cards to all the players. This is called "sporting the Kitty" and is a house rule that is not in the official rules of Bid Whist. It is a questionable practice, because the exposure of the Kitty can allow the opposition to predict the cards retained by the bidder. In competitive Bid Whist, the Kitty is not exposed, and additionally if a player reveals the Kitty or any card in the Kitty, the team loses the hand as a penalty.

---

[57] http://wiki.answers.com/Q/Why are cards set aside in a card game called a Kitty#ixzz22FKsVsTf

The Kitty will often provide support for the winning bidder's hand, as it contains six new cards for the bidder. The cards in the Kitty represent an influx of a fifty percent increase in cards to the bidder (six extra cards). That is the reason why you find many players unadvisedly overbidding their hands to seek help from the Kitty. I do not recommend this strategy because although the Kitty can provide significant help, many times it can destroy a very good hand when it contains six cards that are useless.

This is a caveat that all players should remember. The six cards from the Kitty can be a tremendous help, but when the Kitty contains six cards of your weakest suit then your hand changes from good to bad. Players should bid their hand using the indicating bid from their partner, when possible. It is always better to rely upon your partner's indication of strength, because the cards in the Kitty have backs on them, and you will never know what the Kitty holds until you look at it. Beware of the bad Kitty that can bring devastation to your hand!

The Jokers

The Jokers are an important part of Bid Whist. When the Joker cards were created, Bid Whist and Euchre were the only card games that used the two cards. The two Jokers are the highest-ranking trump cards in Bid Whist, with the Big Joker outranking the Little Joker. The Jokers in most playing card decks will be distinguishable by the color accents on each Joker.

Some brands of cards have one Joker accented with red marks, and that card is the Big Joker. The other Joker has black accent marks and is the Little Joker. Other brands may have one Joker that has a greater image than the other one, and the card with the larger image is the Big Joker. However, some card manufacturers produce a deck with two identical Jokers, and in that instance, players use a marker to write the words Big Joker and Little Joker on those cards.

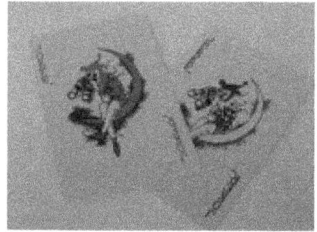

Now that we have reviewed these two key components of the game, we can move to a discussion on the different variations of the game, and then review the rules of the game.

Game Variations

Bid Whist is a card game played by four persons divided into two teams. Each player sits across the table from their partner in an East-West, North-South style. The game uses a standard deck of playing cards consisting of fifty-two cards and to Jokers (fifty-four cards total). They originally used the rules of the Whist game,[58] and later they incorporated many of the rules of Bridge. The principles of play and penalties were the same.[59]

---

[58] (American whist League, 1891)
[59] (Rules of Card Games: Bid Whist, n.d.) (Keiley, 1859) (Agee, 1981)

A Review of the Game's Components

The game of Bid Whist follows the theory of random distribution of cards and the use of teamwork strategies to enable one team to capture more books than the opposing team. There are four preferred game formats that account for most games played today in the United States.

No Kitty Game

This is my game of preference. In different regions, the game's name is "Guts," "Strength of your Hand," or "No Kitty." I have a fondness for this game because it curtails many of the bluffs and opportunities for deception that are available in the six-card Kitty game.

This is the reason we began to play with no Kitty. Players quickly realized they could not discard losers into the Kitty, and the players no longer bid madly for the supporting crutch from the Kitty. It took a very short time until the bids began to be at the one and two level, and some players passed to start the bidding. The game became fun again, and everyone had a reasonable opportunity to bid or pass. There was no longer a five or six level bid by the time it got to 3rd position.

If a player masters the No Kitty game, that player will be successful in all the other games because this game develops your strategy skills. You need a good understanding of the game. You must know how to count cards, how to involve your partner's strong suit, and how to bid your hand. Players need strong Bid Whist techniques in the No Kitty game. The random distribution of the cards can have an impact, but you rely on skill to maneuver through the random distribution factor.

Four-Card Kitty Game

This game is the beginning level of game versions that use a Kitty. The rules are the same, but it establishes the use of a four-card Kitty awarded to the winning bidder. This game does not usually use the Jokers, but some regions replace two cards from the deck with the Jokers. When the Jokers are used, then they are the highest-ranking cards. If the Jokers are not used, the Ace becomes the dominant card in a suit. The winning bidder may select to use any or all of the cards in the Kitty, but must discard and reduce his hand to twelve cards before playing.

Five-Card Kitty Game

The five-card Kitty is the mid-level of game versions that use a Kitty. In this game, the Joker replaces one card. The Joker then becomes the highest-ranking card. The winning bidder must select which cards from the Kitty to use and reduce his hand to twelve cards before playing.

Six-Card Kitty Game

This is the most popular version of Bid Whist played in America, and it uses all of the cards in the deck. This game offers the greatest flexibility of the Bid Whist games because it uses a six-card Kitty to incorporate all fifty-four cards in the deck. The game version is very popular because it allows the winning bidder to supplement his hand with six additional cards.

House Rule Variations for Faster Games

Sometimes a Bid Whist game can last an hour or more when the two opposing teams have equal experience. Matches between two such teams may last twenty or more hands and consume a great deal of time. This can be frustrating for other players waiting to get a match. This precipitated the introduction of faster paced Bid Whist games. Today, many clubs have adapted new and faster games that capture the true "Rise and Fly" spirit to allow everyone a chance to play more often.

In some regions of the country, the need for faster play also led to changes in penalties for infractions. For example, in some regions, you forfeit the game in the event of a renege. This penalty was never in the original rules of the game. However, this rule has become acceptable in many areas to facilitate faster play. The need for quicker games also resulted in special "tournament rules" being created for major events. When you play in other states or in tournaments, it is best to inquire about the rules before you begin your match.

Today, there are three versions of Bid Whist that have gained popularity. Each of the new versions uses the rules and basic structure of Bid Whist. Progressive and Two Bad Bids are two game versions which offer speedier play. Not all of the new games are faster. Minnesota is the latest offspring of Bid Whist, and it is actually more time-consuming than the other games.

Progressive Game

Under the rules of the "progressive game," you will receive your score for achieving your bid. However, if you are "set," you will receive a negative score for your bid, and the other team gets credit for the number of the bid you failed to achieve.[60] Another

---

[60] A team is "set" if they fail to successfully make their bid.

progressive game variation gives the score to the other team if your team is set, and your team's score remains at even. In this game version, no team ever goes in the hole.

Two Bad Bids

Under the rules of the "Two Bad Bids," a team wins the game when they reach seven points or when the opposing team is set twice in the game. The game does not keep a running score, and the teams usually define their score as being "On Board" or having "One Bad Bid." If a team is "On" and they make another bid, they win. If a team acquires "One Bad Bid" and they are set for a second time, they lose the game. If a team makes any two bids during the game, they win; if they are set twice, they lose. This game has a minimum bid level of four, which eliminates the need to keep a point score. This is the preferred game when fast game resolutions are required, or many people are waiting to play.

Minnesota Whist

This exciting new game does not use the Jokers. This game is truly a hybrid because it removes the Jokers, the Kitty, and the Downtown bid. The game is a No Trump game, with the cards played in the Uptown mode. This can be a long match because it requires fourteen points to win the game. This is a No Kitty game, and it has a unique feature—a team can score points for winning fewer books than their opponents win. The game allows the players to select a GRAND option, which means the team that wins six or more books will score points; alternatively, the players can choose the PASS option, where the team winning fewer than seven books will score points. Minnesota has become very popular with online players. The game offers opportunities for teams to score points, even if they have a bad hand.

CHAPTER NINE
A Review of the Original Rules

You will find that the rules in Bid Whist vary across the country. Very few earlier books speak to this subject. This is possibly because of the lack of captured history of the game. In an earlier chapter, I discussed how the game played today is a hybrid game of Whist and Bridge developed by our slave ancestors. It was not permissible for slaves to write, and those Free Blacks with composition skills found difficulty getting articles published. When you consider this fact, you understand why this presented an enormous challenge to Blacks attempting to capture in writing the details of Bid Whist. In the years prior to 1970, the playing rules of Bid Whist were consistent and aligned closely to the standard rules of Bridge. The lack of written information has caused the dilution of the rules of Bid Whist through the years. The lack of a standard nationwide set of playing rules has presented a major challenge to many Bid Whist players.

Bid Whist originally involved a much longer match play time than the present-day game found in most areas across the country. The original game play involved in and out of the hole scoring, which often required over twenty or more deals to complete the match. Today's players have morphed the rules to facilitate faster games. The many rule changes have had an impact on the game's evolution. These rule changes that vary from the original rules of the game are called "House Rules." House Rules vary from state to state, sometimes even intrastate. This presents a challenge to players who are new to an area and playing there for the first time.

Playing the Game

1. The highest bidder wins the Kitty and then selects twelve of the eighteen available cards from the Kitty and their hand. The bidder discards the remaining six cards by placing them face down on the table to form the first book of the game. The bidder does not show the original Kitty nor the discarded Kitty to the other players. The game begins with the winning bidder playing any card of their choice.

2. Each player plays a card in turn. After the bidder's lead card, the play moves clockwise around the table until all four players have played on a book. The winner of that book selects the lead card for the next book.

3. Each player must be able to view each card played and is entitled to spread the cards on the table for viewing purposes.

4. Each book is closed prior to playing the lead card for the next book. A player may request to review the cards while a book remains open, but once the book closes, the book remains closed except to call a renege.

5. All cards must remain in your hand, unexposed, until it is your turn to play.

6. A card played on a book must remain on the table, unless it would force a renege. If a card is exposed accidentally or recovered to prevent a renege, that card can be called from the players at any time by the opposing team when that card's suit is played or when the offending player is placed into a position that a cut is imminent.

7. A trump always beats any non-trump cards played in a book, regardless of the trump's value. If there is more than one trump played, then the highest-valued trump played will win the book.

8. If the winning bid is a No Trump, the highest-valued card in the suit that led wins the book.

9. Jokers have no value in a No Trump bid, and players must discard them immediately when a player no longer has a card of the suit played.

10. In hands where the bidder has a Joker (or Jokers) playing a No Trump bid, the player must place any Jokers in the discard pile (Kitty). If the bidder fails to discard the Joker, the bidder cannot play the Joker as a lead card; the player must either discard the Joker during play or hold it to the last card.

11. If a non-bidding player playing a No Trump bid leads a Joker, the suit of the card played by the player to the immediate left becomes the lead suit. All subsequent players must follow suit if possible.

12. Play each hand out completely.

13. Books must be stacked neatly and separately. One player should keep all the books for each team.

14. A player may call a renege at any time before the mixing of the books together. The penalty for a renege is three books. If a called renege is invalid, then the team that called the renege will be penalized three books.

The Deal

1. The first prerequisite before starting the game is to determine who will be the initial dealer. In most games, one person will shuffle the cards and place them on the table for the cut. After the cut, the dealer distributes the cards in clockwise order until one person receives a Jack. That person receiving the first Jack begins the game as the starting dealer. This is the most preferred method for selection of the dealer, but this process varies in different regions of the country. There are other methods used, such as pulling for the high card, or having the person receiving the first Heart become the dealer.

2. When starting with a new deck, the first dealer will check to see that the Big and Little Jokers are in the deck and that there are no instructional cards in the deck. The dealer should check to see that there are no cards face up in the deck. To prevent a misdeal, the first dealer should verify the deck contains fifty-four playing cards, including the two Jokers.

3. Each new deal requires a shuffle. The cards must be shuffled face down. The dealer will not look at the cards on the bottom of the deck at any time during his shuffling. After the shuffling of the cards, the player on the dealer's right cuts the cards. The player cuts the cards by removing a minimum of four cards or more from the deck to create two stacks. Neither the top nor the bottom cards may remain the same as before the cut.

4. The player on the right should perform a standard square cut (separating the deck into two stacks by removing a portion of the cards from the top of the deck). The player or the dealer switches the bottom cards to the top of the pile to re-form the deck. The dealer cannot begin the deal until the person making the cut places both sections together.

5. The dealer may begin the dealing of the cards after they have been cut. The dealer begins to deal consecutive cards from left to right, starting with the player to his immediate left. The dealer cannot skip a player or otherwise change the normal clockwise distribution of the cards. The dealer must always get the last card. The dealer must not look at the bottom of the deck or look at the faces of any card while dealing, except to identify a booked card.[61] The dealer must exercise care not to expose any of the cards to the other players while dealing. The player deals the cards at a height of no more than 3 inches above the table surface. During the game, the cards must remain above the table at all times.

6. Before the completion of each deal, the dealer must also establish the Kitty in the middle of the table, consisting of six cards from the deck. The six Kitty cards go to the person with the highest bid as a supplement to the player's hand. When establishing a Kitty, the dealer should not place any of the first four cards or the last four cards in the Kitty. The dealer cannot place six consecutive

---

[61] A card in the deck that has been inserted facing upward.

cards in the Kitty. The Kitty must remain on the table at all times until awarded to the winning bidder.

7. Upon completion of the deal, all players must count the number of cards they received to make certain that they have received twelve cards before the bidding begins.

8. In the event of a misdeal, the dealer must re-deal. A misdeal is:

- A player did not receive twelve cards.

- A player has too few or too many cards at the end of a hand.

- More than one card is turned face-up during the deal

- The first four or the last four cards were placed in the Kitty.

9. If there is an irregularity that is not a misdeal, the opposing team has the option to request a re-deal or request a penalty assigned. Irregularities are:

- A player playing a card out of rotation.

- A player bidding out of rotation.

- Placing more than or less than six cards in the discard pile and leading a card.

- Going through or exposing turned books.

- Team members talking across the board.

- A player giving signals (verbal or physical).

- Looking at or exposing the Kitty before the bidding process is complete.

- Reneging or making a false accusation against an opponent of reneging.

A Review of the Original Rules

The above are the basic steps for establishing the first dealer and defining the fundamental process of correctly dealing the cards. Most people are familiar with the term "shady deal," and Bid Whist has other rules and guidelines that help to reduce possible infractions and maintain the integrity of the game.

While on the subject of dealing, let us discuss a common irregularity, and that is having an exposed card in the deck while dealing. The dealer should make every attempt to make sure all the cards are face-down before dealing. However, sometimes while dealing, a card inadvertently may turn face-up, or one or more cards appear in the deck face up. If this should occur, then the following rules apply:

- One card turned up—the deal continues.
- Two cards turned up—the opponents can choose to ask for a re-deal.
- Three cards turned up—there must be a reshuffle and re-deal.
- However, it is a re-deal, and the dealer does not change.

It is the responsibility of each player to count their cards and make sure they have twelve cards before the bidding begins. If at any point after the playing of the first card a player does not have enough cards, then the team of the player with the missing card receives a penalty. The team will either lose their bid or credit a successful bid to the opponents (even if that team may not have been able to make the bid under normal playing of the hand). This rule provides a remedy for those players who may decide to drop a card on the floor when the hand is going adversely for their team.

Beginning the Bidding Process

After the dealing of all the cards and the Kitty, the bidding begins with the player to the immediate left of the dealer. These are the steps for correctly announcing a bid:

1. Bids must range in number from three to seven, with the same three designations for every number. Those designations are:

- Uptown: The player intends to use a trump and declare a trump suit with high cards having the dominant rank if the player wins the bid. A valid number between three and seven must precede the bid.

- Downtown: The player intends to use a trump and declare a trump suit with low cards having the dominant rank if the player wins the bid. A valid number between three and seven must precede the bid.[62]

- No Trump: The player intends to play without a trump with the card direction declared only if the player wins the bid. A valid number between three and seven must precede the bid.

- Pass: A player who chooses not to bid may exercise the option to pass. Any player, except the dealer when the other three bidders have already passed, can exercise this option. When the previous three players have each passed, the dealer is required to place a minimum bid of three or greater.

2. Bids made at the same number level rank from Uptown to Downtown to No Trump, with a No Trump bid holding the highest rank at each number level. The minimum acceptable bid is

---

[62] The terms "Special" and "Low", in some regions indicate a Downtown bid.

three Uptown, and bids cannot exceed seven No Trump.

3. Each successive bidder must either bid higher than any prior bid or elect to pass.

4. After the bidding is complete, the highest bidder wins the bid and the Kitty.

5. The Kitty remains unexposed (sported) on all bids.

6. The player to the left of the dealer begins the bidding process. Each successive player will either bid or elect to pass.

7. All bids must be audible to all players.

8. Players may only ask a member of the opposing team to recant the order of bids.

Completing the Bidding Process

Each player can make one bid with the dealer having the last bid. If each of the first three players passes, the dealer must bid. The player placing the highest bid wins the right to the Kitty. The winning bidder then announces the trump suit or direction for a No Trump bid. The bidder next picks up the Kitty and may choose to use any or none of the Kitty cards to strengthen his hand.

The bidder selects six throwaway cards from the total eighteen cards and places those six cards face-down on the board as the discarded Kitty. The Kitty remains unexposed during the deal and the play of the hand. Some regions play "sport the Kitty,"[63] but this should be discouraged. The showing of the Kitty destroys the secrecy of the Kitty and often gives an advantage to the opponents, as it may indicate what cards the bidder will keep in their hand.

─────────────

[63] A game version that requires the winning bidder to display the Kitty cards to the other players before consolidating the cards into his hand.

Play of the hand can now begin. Before the playing of the first card to the board, the bidder has the option to return to the Kitty and make additional changes to the hand. Once the bidder leads a card, the Kitty becomes closed and not re-opened unless it is determined the dealer does not have the required number of cards. Occasionally, the dealer will either place too many or not enough cards in the Kitty. If this happens, the players must identify the Kitty and count the cards in the Kitty book. The Kitty is always the first book, but if the books have been improperly stacked, then the players can review each book to identify that book as the Kitty.

Scoring – In and Out of the Hole Method

This is the standard and preferred method of scoring used in all of the above games. A team receives a plus score (equal to the number of books won) if they make a bid, or a minus score (equal to the number of their bid) for each set. No Trump bids count for double points. The game continues as each team maintains a running score either plus or minus until one team reaches a positive score of seven for the win or a team reaches a negative score of seven, which constitutes a loss. This is a longer game, but it affords each team the opportunity to maneuver by using both offensive and defensive strategies during the game.

Each team starts at zero (Even Board). The object of the game is for a team to win by scoring seven positive points (above zero) for your team, or to force your opponents to incur seven negative points (below zero). A team that has a negative score is In the Hole. In the game of Bid Whist, each book counts for one point in a standard Uptown or Downtown bid, and in a No Trump bid each book counts for two points. <u>A team cannot accumulate points until after they have won six books during a hand</u>. A team successfully makes a bid if their total number of books won, minus six, is equal to or greater than their bid. Example: A team that bids five must win eleven books (11 - 6) to make their bid. A team that bids three must win nine books (9 - 6) to make their bid.

If the winning bidders make their bid, they win points for the hand. If they fail to make their bid, it reduces their team's score by an amount equal to their bid. A team must win enough books over six to match their bid number. The failure of a team to win the required number of books results in a set, and a negative reduction in their score that equals their stated bid.

If a team is successful in a No Trump bid, they will receive twice the number of points they achieved in the hand. The opposing team cannot score points for a set, even if they win more than six books.

There are a few different scoring systems regionally. The regional differences are minimal and can be quickly absorbed if a player understands the overall game.

CHAPTER TEN
Playing Together as a Team

B id Whist is a game that requires two card players to engage in partnership play. It is important for successful match play that team members understand or have a feel for both the bid and playing style of their partner. This part of the game has never changed in any version of the game. The game of Bid Whist requires the two players on the same team to work collaborative-ly. When two team members are harmonious, it is truly a beautiful thing.

Good Bid Whist players adapt to each other!

There are always game situations when you ask yourself how did those two players do that? They must be cheating because they both had a handful of trumps, or the bidder's partner had more trumps than the bidder did! Conversely, how could that player have known to lead that card or 'skate' on that book? I am not saying that there are not situations where signals or other techniques are used that are against the rules. However, you must understand that although some plays are pure luck, others are examples of excellent evaluation of the possible cards held by you and your partner. Never rush to judgment that a team is using signals or cheating.

Photo: Artist rendition of Cat and the Skunk by Enoch Wilson, Milwaukee, WI.

I have played some great hands and accomplished miraculous sets and saves without strong cards. This happens when you and your partner both understand the hands and play with each other. If your partner shows Hearts, then play the Hearts unless you have key winners to play, or you feel your partner is trying to discard losers. Sometimes when you play your partner's suit, you may have no strength in the suit; however, you should play the best card you have. In a downtown bid, playing a four from your hand can be a powerful pusher, especially if your partner has the Ace with the three or five. The key element in playing with your partner is not trying to dominate the hand if your partner is the winning bidder. Trust your partner and send back your partner's lead when possible, or play the indicator suit your partner may have shown.

When you play as a team, each player must remember not to attempt to be a superhero in all situations. There are two ways to win the match: either by your team achieving a positive score of seven or the other team reaching a negative score of seven. It should be your objective to beat the other team out the front door,[64] and it is frustrating when your team unnecessarily beats the other team out the back door.[65]

One example I will share with you occurred during a game where both teams were even board, and I opened with a four Downtown. The second player proceeded to bid six Uptown. My partner bid six No Trump, and expectedly, the dealer passed. Now

[64] Out the front door is a term used when a team wins the game with a positive score of seven or more points.
[65] Out the back door is a term used when a team loses the game with a negative score of seven or more points.

the big surprise came when my partner announced the direction as Uptown. My partner's first play was the five of Spades. I had the Ace, Jack, and deuce of Spades. I played the Ace and played the Jack of Spades back. The Jack turned, and I then played the deuce of Spades. My partner won the book and led a Club. I played the King of Clubs, which turned, and I immediately played Clubs back. Most surprising to me was that my partner went on to make the bid, only losing the last book.

Some players want to be heroic when it is not necessary. However, they flirt dangerously with beating the opponent out of the back door. The numerous gaps in my partner's hand reflected questionable bidding strategy in this situation.

A review of the bids indicated it was not required for my partner to take any action. I indicated a Joker with my bid. If my partner holds two Aces, then our team has an eighty percent chance of setting the opponents' bid and a ninety-five percent chance of turning the one book needed to stop a Boston.

It is questionable strategy when a player opts to bid a six No Trump with only two Aces, and without a solid run suit. The player decided to go in a direction away from his partner's strength. My partner failed to consider the opposing player's bid in 2nd position. If the opponent did not have a strong Uptown hand, he would only bid a five Uptown, knowing that his partner had the last bid.

My partner totally disrespected this bidder and opened the door for disaster. Miraculously, he made the bid, but I had to turn three books for him. A review of the hand shows my partner was missing the ♠AJ, ♣K, ♥K, and had no Diamonds. In my opinion, this was a terrible bid. It saved our opponents from taking an obvious defensive set, and put us in the hazardous position of losing the game on the first hand.

My partner bragged and talked trash for several minutes. However, from my viewpoint, it convinced me that I would not be comfortable with the player as a partner. I have no objections to my partner bidding a six No Trump and disregarding my Joker, but I expected him to have a much stronger hand. Our team was not in danger of losing the game at that point. The No Trump bid in this situation could have been disastrous.

Each partner should play defensively when necessary, and consistently consider the impact of the bid or non-bid of your partner. You must consider the odds that your opponents can go out with their bid based on your cards and the indicated support from your partner.

An example of teamwork is each team member making an effort to identify his or her strong suit. If I show a Heart, it does no good in most instances when my partner also shows a Heart. It is up to the other partner to show the suit they intend to protect. I share with you the story when in 1st position I bid a four No Trump. Our opponents took me out with a five Downtown.

My hand was ♥A743 ♣ A74 ♦Q ♠J543. The bidder named Diamonds as trumps and when I ran out of trumps, I showed a Heart. My partner on the next round indicated a Heart and continued to discard Hearts on most of the ensuing Diamonds. Our opponents had a long run in Diamonds, and the bidder played down to the last four cards. At this time, I had no idea of what to hold, so based on my partner's discard, I threw down to the ♣A, ♥A, ♠34. It turned out my partner had all the Clubs but the Ace and nothing on the Hearts. The bidder had the Spades and went on to make a Boston. I can fault myself also for my discard because I could have thrown away the Ace of Hearts to protect the other two suits; however, my partner's discards confused me.

This story emphasizes that good teamwork can sometimes save the day. If my partner had indicated Clubs, perhaps I could have seen that our opportunity existed in the Spades. It is possible I would not have made that astute observation, but a major crack in the armor of any team occurs when players distrust the discard of their partner. It becomes difficult in future hands to interpret what support your partner can offer.

A player must realize that if he/she has a powerful hand, it is likely their partner has a relatively poor hand. If the defensive position partner is using good strategies, then the partner must make a protective bid of five or better to protect the team. When you have the first bid, any false bid you place on the board will affect all players, including possibly your partner. Whenever you offer a counterfeit bid in the opening position, you are lying to all the players—including your partner! This illustration should serve as a reminder that a false bid in 1st position travels to all players, including your partner.

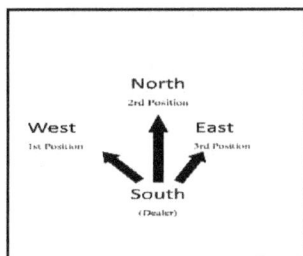

North
2nd Position

West
1st Position

East
3rd Position

South
(Dealer)

I offer the story of when I was playing with a new partner, and our opponents were four in the hole, while our team was even board. My partner passed in 1st position. My hand held the following cards ♥1087 ♣ 654 ♦8 ♠J9654

Not having a Joker or an Ace, I bid six Downtown. The Kitty was ugly, with all middle cards. I was satisfied with my bid because I believed it was the proper defensive move to save the game. It was during the play of the hand that I discovered my partner had both Jokers and three Aces, and passed. I had taken a major set for no reason.

Your chances of winning increase when you play as a team. Some hands make it difficult to bid in the 1st position. Occasionally, you might find yourself with ten cards of the same suit, but you are missing key cards in your trumps. Your other two cards are winners, but you do not have a Joker. This becomes a difficult decision, and it may be better for you to pass in 1st position. However, if you wish to play the hand, then push the bid to the six level. If the opponents take out the bid, your partner will need to turn two books to set. It is unlikely that you will turn a book. There is still an inherent danger even at the six level, because your partner might misinterpret your bid and push it to a six No Trump or six Downtown.

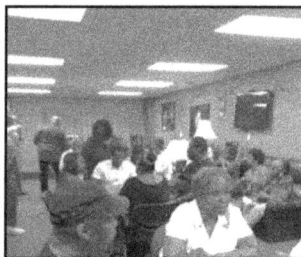

The concept of team play increases your winning percentage.

Each team member must understand and use the team strategies that offer the best opportunities for success. It requires both team members to be coordinated. As an example, let us examine the Trapping of the Ace strategy. The strategy is very successful when your partner has bid a standard bid indicating a Joker, and the opponents have bid a No Trump.

Trapping the Ace

For illustration purposes, you are in 3rd position, and the following were prior bids:

1st position   4 Uptown

2nd position   5 No Trump

3rd position   6 Uptown – (your defensive bid)

4th position   Pass

You must bid defensively to protect your team, but many times these bids have excellent chances if you have a Joker, decent high cards, and can get two suited. After discarding the Kitty, you hold the following cards: BJ♥Q109765 ♠KQJ109.

This hand does not appear to be an adequate hand for a successful bid, but consider the following strategy. The odds are 3-1, and the ♥A is in the hand of the 2nd position player. You should play your cards based on the   assumption the 2nd position player holds the trump Ace. Your first card played should be ♥7, to solicit the Joker from your partner. Your partner should then return the trumps with his highest remaining trump, and you are hopeful your partner has the ♥K to play back. You should not cover the King when played because you predict the No Trump bidder holds the Ace. If the King clears the board, you can only hope your partner has another Heart to play. If your partner has another Heart, you are very possibly on your way to a successful bid. On the third play of trumps, you would play your Queen and lead back with your Little Joker, which should capture all the outstanding trumps. This would leave you with only one loser, the ♠A, and you will have used your team resources to turn a defensive bid into a successful outcome.

It is the team strategy and understanding of the game that opens the doors of opportunity. If your partner did not have the ♥K, your chances of success diminish. Some players would opt not to play back the King, not understanding the importance of leading that card through the No Trump bidder.

This illustrates my last point. It is important, when possible, to choose a partner who complements your style of play. Most Bid Whist players are very competitive, but there are many who play strictly for the fun. My experience has been that those two styles will not match up well. The competitive player is intent on winning and the partner just wants to have some fun.

I welcome and support those players who just want to enjoy the game. The game needs the participation of the casual player, and highly competitive players should occasionally relax. It is great when seasoned players devote the time to share the game with newbies. Typically, it ends badly when a competitive player and a fun player team together. The combination of the two styles, as a rule, will have a high losing percentage and can become a trash talker's dream as the mismatched team loses consistently. It can still be a lot of fun, even if the losers have to laugh at themselves.

Now that I have mentioned trash talking, I would be remiss if I did not add remarks about the subject. This humorous aspect of the game has consistently been a part of Bid Whist over the years. However, the younger generation of players has taken trash talking to a new level to which I take exception. Trash talking in earlier days was a verbal spanking or ridicule delivered in relatively good taste. Trash talking was impromptu and humorous remarks that exhibited the card players' quick wit at adapting jovial comments to one of the plays that occurred during the last game. Today I have seen too many instances where extreme vulgarity has been the core of trash talking. This disturbs me greatly, and I hope that my remarks in this book might serve as a reminder to players to minimize the use of vulgarity.

Extreme profanity and abusive language are not the same as trash talking and should have no place in Bid Whist. I understand that the younger generation has a different outlook and that for some members of their generation, profanity has become a part of their culture. However, I hope this part of the new generation's culture does not continue to cross over into Bid Whist. A long tirade of profanity is not a display of intelligence or wit. In most games of sport, a player receives an ejection or penalty for uttering extreme profanity.

Profanity does not help to elevate the popularity of the game. Our ancestors created Bid Whist as a connector for maintaining unity, establishing new relationships, bonding, and relieving the stress of everyday adversity. I hope newer Bid Whist players will strive to maintain the game's high enjoyment level and spirit of competitive entertainment with respect and civility.

CHAPTER ELEVEN
The Art of Bidding

The illustration on the left shows the standard seating patterns for each player. This chart will serve as a reference as we discuss bidding and the different player positions. The deal rotates to each player; however, for illustration purposes only, the dealer will remain in the South seat.

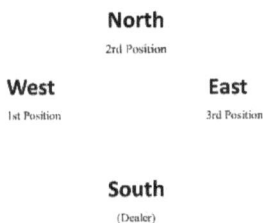

1. Bidding begins with the player to the immediate left of the dealer and moves around the table in a clockwise rotation. There are five number levels (three through seven) used in bidding, and each level has three classifications (Uptown-Downtown-No Trump) that must be declared with the number level. Each player receives one bid, and that bid cannot be withdrawn or changed unless the bidder has duplicated a bid previously given by another bidder. In such instances, the player who duplicated an earlier bid must increase their bid up one level while maintaining their bid direction and Trump/No Trump selection. The dealer always re-

North
2rd Position

West
1st Position

East
3rd Position

South
(Dealer)

ceives the last opportunity to bid. This is the standard ranking of bids, from the lowest to the highest:

•	3 Uptown	3 Downtown	3 No Trump
•	4 Uptown	4 Downtown	4 No Trump
•	5 Uptown	5 Downtown	5 No Trump
•	6 Uptown	6 Downtown	6 No Trump
•	7 Uptown	7 Downtown	7 No Trump

2. Bid Whist games that use a Kitty have a minimum bid of three or higher. The high bid in all games is seven, with a seven No Trump being the highest allowable bid. A player cannot bid higher than seven No Trump. Games played without a Kitty have a minimum bid of one. If a player bids below the minimum, they must increase the number to the required minimum. They cannot change their original direction or Trump/No Trump selection. They cannot withdraw their bid. This rule is to maintain the integrity of the game and to prevent inappropriate signals of the player's cards. If a bidder passes, they can only state the word "Pass." They cannot say, "I pass a four No Trump," or anything similar that might be a verbal signal. This would be an infraction. A violation of this nature allows the opponents the option for a re-deal as a penalty for this infraction.

3. When a player bids, they must declare a number level, followed by their card direction designation.

Example 1:

North Player seat: I bid Four Downtown.

East Player seat: I bid Five Uptown.

South Player seat: I bid Five No Trump.

West Player seat: Pass.

The player in the South seat has placed the highest bid. The player wins the Kitty and the right to name whether the direction of the cards will be played up or down.

Example 2:

North Player seat: I bid Three Downtown.

East Player seat: Pass.

South Player seat: I bid Five No Trump.

West Player seat: I bid Six Uptown.

The West position was the highest bidder. The West seat wins the Kitty and the right to name the trump suit. The card ranking is Uptown, the direction named in the bid.

All standard bids except a No Trump must indicate a direction, and if that bid should win, the direction will not change. The winning bidder can select the trump suit. The winner of a No Trump bid may select the direction of the cards, but they cannot designate a trump suit. This bidding process gives each player an opportunity to manage their cards by placing a bid appropriate for the cards in their hand. Players attempt to leverage the strength of their cards for either launching an offensive maneuver or establishing a better defensive position.

Positional Bidding

Players who understand the positional bidding strategy of Bid Whist will usually have a high winning percentage. These players will attack or defend, as the situation dictates. Each team has

an opening bidder and a closing bidder, and they each have responsibilities throughout the game. The opening bidders are the West & North players, and they occupy the 1st and 3rd positions. The closing bidders sit in the East & South seats, in the 2nd and 4th positions. Each player can be an offensive weapon during the bidding process, but the closing bidders have the defensive responsibilities for their team. The 3rd and 4th seats make the final decision on whether a pass or high bid is in the team's best interest.

The act of appropriately bidding is a learned skill, and so is the adept use of the option to pass. Each hand in the game is important, and most games are not won or lost on the first hand. However, it can be a pivotal point in the game. Your team's strategy will vary throughout the game, and your team may switch from an offensive posture to a defensive stance. Your team's beginning movements will have an influence on your team's strategy for the ensuing hands.

A successful outcome at this point can put your team in a position of strength. If your team makes this bid, then your team has the potential to win the game on the next hand. Consequently, if you set your opponent's initial bid, your team will be poised to win the game by setting the opponent's bid.[66] Therefore, the results of the first hand dictate the defensive or offensive stance required for the ensuing hand.

---

[66] (Greg Morrison, 2005)

Positional bidding is important at all times. However, the second hand is when one of the team is in a position of advantage. The most frequent mistakes made by players in non-threatening situations are the failure to exercise a good bidding opportunity, an exaggerated bid from the opening position, and poor decisions in discarding the Kitty cards.

Let us examine some of the problems with an improper opening bid. I have played hands where my partner had both Jokers and two Aces, and passed in 1st position. The second player either bid or passed. However, it is the responsibility of the 3rd position player to protect the game. When I find myself in 3rd position with only a couple of possible winners, I usually end up bidding five down or six down, because I am trying to survive and get to the next hand. If my partner had bid, it may not have changed my final decision, but it would have allowed me to evaluate our possible team strength and make a more informed decision.

In this particular instance, my partner had four Aces and both Jokers. The strong hand of my partner could not save me because I had a poor hand. Imagine my frustration when I discovered my partner had forced me to bid for the hole out of fear that the other team had all the cards my partner failed to indicate. Our team was now unnecessarily in a precarious position in the hole. Team communication via positional bidding might have prevented the situation.

It is unwise to pass in 1st position if your hand contains a Joker and two Aces, two Aces, or a Joker and one Ace. You do not have to place a strong bid at this point. However, you should indicate that you have some defensive stoppers. A bid in 1st position does not offer a guarantee that your partner will not panic and over bid. However, it will give your partner some options to consider. It is possible that your partner may still feel the need for a protective bid, but you will have indicated some defensive support. If your team is not in the hole, and you pass in 1st position with several good cards, you have put your partner into a three-against-one situation. These are bad odds and usually end in your team's defeat.

Alternately, there is a greater mistake than passing in 1st position with good cards. It is placing an opening bid with no ranking cards. A player who bids in 1st position is indicating the possession of an Ace or Joker, depending on the bid. The partner may have cards that are in the same indicated direction and may develop a false sense of confidence, expecting support from the partner's hand. This type of bidding miscommunication could end badly because the defending partner may pass or push a higher bid based on the partner's false bid.

I recall one experience that might serve to highlight the importance of not sending a false bid in 1st position. It was the opening bid of a new match, and my partner started with a five Downtown. The first opponent passed, and I bid a six Uptown. I held in my hand before the Kitty:

LJ♥AKQJ1098 ♣A ♦AK10. My ego began talking, and I started to bid seven Uptown. I also considered bidding six or seven No Trump. The Kitty gave me one more heart. I discarded the losing Diamond, and my hand was locked with only one loser—the Big

Joker. I triumphantly announced I had a Boston, and I played the eight of Hearts. The opponent played the Big Joker on the book and laughed at me. My partner sent a five Downtown bid without a Joker or an Ace. I still made my bid because of the superior strength of my hand, but I had exposed myself to a potential set because my partner had made a high bid with no supporting major cards.

This illustrates why you should never give a bid that can misrepresent your hand to your partner when you are in 1st position. In even board situations, a 1st position bid from your partner may allow you to pass bids that otherwise might present a strong danger. You can often pass bids because you know your partner has an Ace or Joker, and with your cards, the other team can be set. Even if they make the bid, there is not a clear danger of them running seven. Bid Whist is a complex game, and these things are not hard truths, but you try to play the odds and probabilities.

A key strategy for the player in 3rd or 4th position is <u>do not take an unreasonable chance that will lose the game for your team on this hand.</u> If there is a reasonable doubt, it is best to exercise one of two available options. If you are the dealer, you should take out the opponent's bid if it does not put you out the back door. If you are in 3rd position, make the highest possible push bid that will not push your team out of the back door.

Many players fail to take out the opponent's bid, even if they are even board, because they have terrible cards. If you are not playing a form of progressive bid, then a player should bid defensively. If your team is even board, the other team cannot go out if you bid seven. Even if they turn all the other books, the Kitty will always be your book. Your team may only turn one book, but it stops the other team from making seven. You still will have another deal, and one more chance to get a good hand.

I have one caution for players when playing with new partners for the first time. Every player will make mistakes or sometimes have a lapse in good judgment that results in the loss of a game. However, an occasional mistake might not be indicative of the player's overall game skills. Players should never quickly attribute one or two bad decisions by another player as poor playing skills. The cards "have backs on them" and some judgment calls are the result of a bad bid or pass from their partner. Players should give their partner the benefit of the doubt until further recurrences may establish that the player truly does have underdeveloped game skills.

I have played over twenty-five thousand games at different online sites. I always played under an assumed name, but this book will destroy my anonymity, so now I will have to find another alias. My two favorite websites are Case's Ladder Online and the Whistportal.com. Many of the mobile and online sites have frequent software glitches, and I have found these two sites to be among the most reliable. I enjoy playing online because you can play from the comfort of your home, and players are usually available because they live in different national or international time zones.

Playing online at the different sites presents some unique challenges. Your selection of a partner is very random, and new players may have some difficulty finding a partner. You will not have the ability to observe the other players, so you could be playing with a young teenager that is just learning the game. You may be playing with a skilled player who on that day is either very tired or has had too much to drink. In eye-to-eye play, you can size up your partner and the other players by looking for the "tells" that are often easily discernable. <u>Tells</u> are the unconscious mannerisms displayed by some players as they gather their cards and it often reveals information about the strength of their cards. Most experienced players are skilled at looking for these signs, but the online computer game takes away this advantage.

Furthermore, when you play online there is always the probability that one of the players may have a computer malfunction or power outage in the middle of the game. Some players play on the company's computer while at work, so they turn off the computer when the supervisor approaches. These occurrences will, unfortunately, cause the termination of your game.

I remember playing an online game with a player whom I had played with on several occasions, and we had been very successful. However, on this day, it was evident that his game play was very different. I sent an inter-game message inquiring about their unusual play. I was surprised to find that my partner had left the house and assigned their daughter to finish the game for them. Then it all became clear why his style of play was so different. I could do nothing but graciously finish the match. However, knowing this fact tempered my frustration, and I did remove this person from my partner list.

Newer players find that the most pressing questions are:

• How do I know what to bid?

• When should I bid?

• When should I pass?

Players should first consider any other bids that occurred in the hand. The player in the opening position should make a bid that has a reasonable chance for success based on the cards held in his or her hand. An opening position player should not overbid with expectations of significant help from their partner. The players in third and fourth position, having received some indication of partner support, may upwardly adjust their bid based on their partner's bid.

Newer players have a tendency to think, "I have no hand and; therefore, I will not bid under any circumstance." However, the overall game strategy will often require players to make a bid that exceeds the capability of their cards. Players who do not understand which situations require such strategy adjustments will usually have lower winning percentages.

The game presents both offensive and defensive situations. You should develop an understanding of these situations and adjust your bid accordingly. Experienced players will not allow you to draw them into a trap by placing a misdirection bid or passing with strong cards. Seasoned players will allow you to hang yourself with such play. Sometimes you may be able to sell a trash bid; however, a trash bid will only work if your team is on board and the threat of the bid might appear creditable to the opposition.

Players normally bid offensively based on their cards and any indications from their partner. However, other bids fall into the defensive category. Defensive bids are the key to winning a match. If you do not play defense, your odds of winning decrease. I cannot stress enough that playing strong defense will always improve your overall chances of winning the game.

Defensive bids will fall into one of the following categories:

• Defensive or Takeout Bid

• Push Bid

• Indicator Bid

• Supporting Bid

If you understand how to both recognize and use takeout bids, you will increase your winning percentage. Players not only need to know when to use defensive bids for your team's sake, but your opponents will also use protective strategies, and players need to recognize the situation when this happens. If you do not recognize such situations, you may bid defensively against what was a defensive bid attempt from your opponent. When this happens, your team usually suffers.

The players in 1st and 2nd position will either pass, give an indicator bid or offer a strong bid based on their hand. Their bid or pass will indicate to their partner the appropriate defensive or offensive position required.

The defensive responsibility falls upon the players in the 3rd and 4th position. These two players have the final bid for their team. The fate of each team often will rest with these two players. The player who can decipher the bid/pass of their partner in conjunction with the bids of the opponents will make the decision on the strategy needed to either place the team in a position of strength, or position the team for survival mode.

The partner with the last bid will determine whether to bid defensively using a push bid, takeout bid or shutout bid, depending on the team's position on board. That player must also consider the score of the opponents when making the final decision. This will work most effectively when your partner consistently indicates the perceived strength of his hand, without being overly aggressive as the team's first bidder.

Your overall hand will determine if a player will bid a No Trump. However, there may be other factors to consider. Did your partner bid? What are the weaknesses of the hand? Did the opposition indicate any directions? (Remember, sometimes the opposition will place a misdirection bid intended to influence you to go the wrong way!) Usually the first bidder will accurately indicate their hand. Sometimes, you will have a player who possesses a good supporting hand and passes, knowing that they can offer substantial help for their partner and also provide a strong defense if the other team bids. Some players will pass even if they have a Joker or an Ace. I personally dislike having my partner do this because I have no idea how to defend when this happens. I have often had to place a defensive bid of five or even six, only to find that my partner had two Aces or possessed a Joker and an Ace.

CHAPTER TWELVE

Uptown and Downtown Bids

Most players are comfortable with Uptown bids. The uptown hierarchy of the cards is in most card games: Poker, Spades, Hearts, Bridge, Blackjack, etc. Bid Whist offers an opportunity to reverse the ranking order of the cards. Players may find this confusing initially, but they adapt quickly.

The normal ranking order of the cards in Bid Whist is

Big Joker, Little Joker, Ace, King, Queen, Jack,10, 9, 8, 7, 6, 5, 4, 3, and 2.

When the bidder successfully wins the bid with a Downtown bid, the order reverses to Big Joker, Little Joker, Ace, 2, 3, 4, 5, 6, 7, 8, 9, 10, Jack, Queen, and King.

The ranking of the three major cards, Big Joker, Little Joker, and Ace, are the same for either Uptown or Downtown play.

However, in a Downtown Bid the two, three, and four replace the King, Queen, and Jack in the ranking. The hierarchal order of the 5, 6, 7, 8, 9, and 10 also reverses.

In an Uptown bid where the player holds the King and Queen in a suit, the player plays the King to force the Ace to the board. If it is a Downtown bid, the two and three replace the King and Queen in the ranking. The player would play the two to force the Ace.

In a No Trump bid, the Big Joker and Little Joker do not have a ranking. These two cards have no value and cannot win a book. It seldom happens, but if a player leads a Joker in a No Trump, the card has no suit attachment, and the suit determination becomes established by the second player's card. The Jokers become discards. It is unusual, but I have seen on two occasions where the first player played a Joker, and the second player played the other Joker, thus, making the card of the third player the suit indicator for the book. The playing of the second Joker is not a renege, as there is no suit designation until the playing of a suited card to the board. This is only true in a No Trump bid.

Personally, I see no advantage in leading the Joker in a No Trump unless the second player is the bidder and your strategy is to force the bidder into the hand to protect your other cards. This play allows the bidder to regain control as the bidder, or his partner, will play a dominant card from the opening suit on the Joker. It is better to open your team's strong suit. The Joker lead can only be beneficial if the player is attempting to protect a key card.

CHAPTER THIRTEEN
Playing a No Trump Bid

Many players are uncomfortable with playing a No Trump bid. A No Trump will give you double points, but you may be vulnerable if the opposition wins an early book. Newer players are often unsure of when to bid a No Trump, for either defensive or offensive purposes. Many players upon winning the bid do not know how to discard the Kitty to protect their overall hand. Many experienced players do not know how to play a No Trump bid from a defensive posture.

When contemplating bidding a No Trump from your own hand, you need to consider any previous bids. Did your partner bid? Did the opposition indicate any directions? Usually the first bidder will accurately indicate their hand, but any other bids by the opponents can be purposely misdirecting. Sometimes you will have a player holding an excellent supporting hand pass, knowing they can offer strong help for a bid from their partner and provide sufficient defense if the opposition bids. I personally dislike my partner to pass in such situations because if I have the last bid for our team, I have no idea of the best defense for the hand.

Let us address when it might be appropriate to bid a No Trump. If you have the opening bid, and have an Ace and some accompanying support cards in the other suits, a three No Trump might serve as an invite to your partner.

This is not a strong bid, but in some cases, it can help your partner to make the right decision on how to protect the hand by either passing or pushing the bid. Some people feel that a three No Trump is a useless bid because it provides little information, other than your hand possesses an Ace. However, it can be a valid indicator bid if you have at least two other cards that will support your partner either up or down. The value of the three No Trump bid is it conveys to your partner some defensive support against a No Trump from the opponents.

When both teams are even board, it is not often that the opponents will pass your bid. Occasionally, the opponent will bid a four or five No Trump over your bid. This would be an instance when your partner would consider your announcement of an Ace in determining to pass the No Trump overbid from the opponents. However, before placing a three no bid, you need to consider the score. If your opponents are in the hole, the odds increase that the other players will pass on your three no bid. If the opponents are in the hole, then your hand should have adequate support because the other players could pass your bid. An experienced partner may take out your bid if they have little or no support. Players should remember that if you take out your partner with a four bid, your team would only lose four points, in contrast to missing six points for an unsuccessful three No Trump attempt.

One major consideration in bidding a No Trump should be the strategy of how you can control the games with your cards. A No Trump is not like a regular bid in that if you lose control of your suit, you cannot use a trump to cut and regain control. The bidder must consider how to gain re-entry if the cards do not fall. Even if your partner has two or three Aces, you must consider how your partner can return the game to you. Some players bid five No Trump in 1st position with only one Ace, and this can be a disaster. Such a bid is achievable with support from your partner and good communication, but if you lose control and your partner cannot put you in, it becomes a disaster.

When the opening partner has sent a strong No Trump bid, and the other partner has a substantial long suit, some players will push an even higher No Trump bid. They anticipate that they will turn nine or more books and pass it off to the partner to complete the bid. However, if you have five or more losers, it is not wise to anticipate your partner can help you to throw away so many cards. It can happen, but it is risky to bid on a dream. However, it is worth the risk if the opponents have previously scored.

Although the No Trump bid can be challenging for any player, it offers great reward if successfully completed. It is a bid that neither team should take for granted, even if the team that placed the bid is six in the hole. When your opponents are six in the hole, it does relieve some of the pressure, as you only need to turn one book to save the game.

Many players will pass automatically when their opponents bid a No Trump and the opponents are six in the hole. I understand the thinking, but I strongly disagree with using this logic in all situations. If you are the last bidder for your team and your partner did not bid, then you need to consider carefully whether passing the No Trump bid is the best option.

Red Alert!

Red flags should go up and whistles should sound in your head, especially if you have no Aces. Even if you have an Ace, be very cautious if you are missing an entire suit! A player with a long suit of nine or more will destroy most hands. A player holding eleven cards in one suit usually has a guaranteed six No Trump, and such a hand will cause you to discard down to the last one or two cards. When you first viewed your hand and its defensive potential, you believed that you had stoppers in three suits. However, your opponent's long line of one suit will have you gasping for air as you realize you may only turn a book in one suit—but only if you keep the right suit!

No Trump bids require an even greater emphasis on playing as a team. If your teammate has bid the No Trump, never block your partner's path with a key card in your partner's run suit. If you do not have enough cards in the suit to play the suit back, then sacrifice that key card early in the play. For example, your partner declared a No Trump Uptown and played the Ace of Hearts. If you have the Queen and only three Hearts, it is important that on the second Heart book, you discard the Queen. You should not get stuck in the hand on the third book and have nothing to play, nor any idea of what to play if you did have other potential winners.

If your partner bid the No Trump, then he is the leader of the team for the hand. Do not attempt to get in the game early, because you could destroy his strategy and ruin the bid for your partner. If you have support for your partner, you will have the opportunity on the next card to indicate where you might offer support.

No Trump bids can be challenging because very seldom do the cards play out as expected. Many times, you will find you have to make strategy adjustments on the fly. When this occurs, you need to incorporate your partner into the game. It may become necessary for you to turn every book possible from your hand and then play your partner's invite and hope your partner can finish the hand. This should not often happen because you should not bid a No Trump expecting your partner to turn five books. This might occasionally happen, but realistically, you should only expect two or three books from your partner. If you are expecting more from your partner, you should not have bid the No Trump. If you are anticipating help from your partner based on their opening bid or an invite shown by their discard, then you need to set the stage by being prepared to get out of your partner's way before you attempt to put your partner in the hand.

Let us use the example of your partner showing Hearts as an invite and the No Trump is Uptown. If you hold the Ace of Hearts, you must play it before your partner can run Hearts. If you hold the King of Hearts, your partner cannot run Hearts until the King falls. These are very general statements, but they emphasize the need to open up the suit for your partner and be prepared not to block the run of your partner. Sometimes in a No Trump bid, you will play just one key card (Ace or King) for your partner's invite and then resume playing your key suit. This serves as an alert to your partner that you have recognized their invite, and they should be prepared for an entrance later. The caveat is that your partner may not have any support and may only be discarding losers.

No Trump bids are scored as double points, and understandably so because of the complexity of making the bid successfully. A well-executed No Trump is one of the biggest thrills in Bid Whist. The other one is executing a Boston.

CHAPTER FOURTEEN
Defensive Strategies

There is an offense and defense in Bid Whist. You will have a span where you will get bad cards. You might find yourself in a position where you do not feel you can adequately defend against the cards of your opponent. These situations will require you to take a defensive stance to survive the hand. You possibly can regain position with the next hand.

Strategically, it is very acceptable (and often advisable) to bid something you cannot conceivably make. This defensive posture is "taking the set." Taking a set will allow you to play another hand, hoping the next hand will be a good one.

The variation of Bid Whist game you are playing will determine when you can use this strategy. If you are playing standard Bid Whist or "In and Out of the Hole," you will be able to use this defensive ploy. Players seldom use this tactic when playing Two Bad Bids or Progressive.[67] The standard game of Bid Whist offers strategic moves you can use when necessary. If you are even board and the other team is five on board, your best option is to bid six Downtown. If your team is five on board and your opponents are five on board, it may require a bid of seven. This strategy is challenging for many players. They mistakenly pass because they have

---

[67] (Beck, 1994) (Greg Morrison, 2005)

no long run suit[68] or key cards. This defensive strategy may be the only feasible option in some situations.

There are advantages of bidding very high when in doubt. You may discover the other team did not have a strong hand. However, players are not fortune tellers. You can never know when the combined hands of the other team will give them the cards needed to make the Boston. A good Bid Whist player must evaluate their hand with their partner's bid to determine if their team might turn any books. If it is not a No Trump, then you need to turn enough books to keep the other team from winning. I did not say your team had to set the other team's bid, but rather your goal is to prevent them from winning on the current hand. Survival is the key. Your team must hold the line until help arrives in the form of a good hand.

If you are confident the other team cannot go out on the bid, this might not be the time to take a set. That responsibility falls on the last bidder for your team. That player must determine the answer to two questions. The other team is even board; if I pass this bid, can the other team make seven? The other team is in the hole; if they bid a No Trump, can my team turn enough books to stay in the game?

I have been frustrated on many occasions when my partner passed with nothing in their hand. When you have nothing, this should be a warning signal—BID, BID, and BID. Bid as high as possible without pushing your team out of the "back door." Players who pass in the 3rd position with no cards will have a loss per-

---

[68] A run suit or long suit is six or more cards in the same suit.

centage rate of over fifty-five percent. The 4th position player will get a bargain-priced No Trump and win the game, or they might successfully make a low-level standard bid.

The 3rd position player has the obligation to be the defensive back for the team. If your partner has passed, and you hold no winners in your hand, then the good cards are either in the Kitty or in the hands of your opponents. Either of these situations represents a clear and present danger. If you cannot anticipate turning a book, then it is probable that your partner (who has passed) will not turn a book.

When you are Missing an Entire Suit

An equally challenging situation is having strong cards, but missing an entire suit. These circumstances require extreme caution. A player who has a long suit of nine or more cards will destroy even the strongest defensive hand. There are several unwritten rules in Bid Whist, and one of those rules is, "If you are sitting in the defender's seat, bid when you are in doubt!"

In Bid Whist, the art of playing defense is to bend but not break. SURVIVE and stay in the game until the good hand comes. You will not always be able to survive, but it is so exhilarating to come from behind after being six down to win the game. When you feel that joy and excitement, then you will know why Bid Whist players love this game!

CHAPTER FIFTEEN

Basic Strategy Tips

I have covered many of the strategies used in Bid Whist. The following is a list of basics tips that may assist your development of a strong game strategy and improve your winning percentage.

Important Things to Remember:

- DO make it a habit to count the trumps during the play of each hand, even if you are not the winning bidder.

- DO reduce your hand to the least number of suits possible if you have won the bid. It is prudent to discard Kings and deuces in the Kitty to reduce the vulnerability of your hand. No Trump bids may require additional protection.

- DO remember to never over-bid when you are the first bidder. To do so might mislead your partner into making a misguided pass or reinforcing your bid.

- DO defend your team's position if you have the closing bid. It is your responsibility to protect the game for your team.

- DO play your best card first if you only hold two cards in a suit (neither card being the Ace) and a player leads the suit through you. If the opponent has played away from the Ace or your partner has the Ace, this is probably the only chance for that card to turn.

- DO give your partner an indicating bid, if possible.
- DO develop and maintain a consistent style of play.

Finally, newer players should understand that Bid Whist is a card game that has many nuances. It is possible for you to achieve a decent win-loss record if you understand the basic strategies and techniques. Bid Whist is unlike the sports arena where players have mentors and coaches. This seldom occurs in Bid Whist. Many players never listen to the advice and counsel of experienced players. Many long-time Bid Whist players have not taken their game to the next level, and their skills have remained at the novice level of their earlier days.

Developing Discipline

A Chicago newspaper columnist wrote about playing very competitive Bid Whist games with the legendary basketball star, Michael Jordan. Great athletes such as Michael Jordan and Tiger Woods had mentors who worked with them to develop their skills and discipline. Successful people, in all arenas, honed their skills by maintaining discipline, proper form, and consistent execution. Bid Whist requires a degree of discipline and has certain patterns of execution that have proven to be most likely to achieve the desired results. These patterns of play are not always going to be successful, but they will increase your winning percentage significantly over the long run.

New players need to establish individual discipline in their style of play. Some players appear to have unorthodox playing styles, but if you dissect their overall play, you will find that they have developed their unique strategies over time. There is more than one way to play a hand; however, your style of play should employ a consistent strategy for successful outcomes. If you veer from consistency and play a strictly guessing game, you will sporadically win games, but your win-loss statistics will reflect a higher overall loss percentage.

Bid Whist players usually will play the percentages. Good players will review their hand to determine the chances of either making their bid or setting the other team.

The game of Bid Whist is subject to the Laws of Random Distribution of Cards.[69] A better understanding of the random distribution percentages will enable you to take your game to the next level. Players should not blindly bid for the Kitty to get an extra six cards without understanding the odds of the cards you need being either in the Kitty or your partner's hand—or unfortunately in the hand of your opponent. The ability to evaluate the percentage probabilities increases when each partner exercises good communications through proper and accurate positional bidding.

I recommend you select a player who has demonstrated consistent success, and attempt to emulate the personal style of that player. When you have reasonably mastered the style of that player, you can begin to incorporate new tactics into your game. Your

_____

[69] http://www.random.org/

goal should be to achieve a winning percentage rate of fifty-two percent or better, which will establish you as a competent player. Highly skilled players are those who have stepped their game up to above fifty-six percent.[70] Players who achieve the fifty-six percent level can successfully compete with any Bid Whist player, anywhere and anytime. Players above the fifty-six percent level may not win every tournament, but they have established themselves as very competitive and highly respected players.

I am a firm believer that players with strong skills will have the advantage over players who are lucky and get good cards. This is true in most sporting games, and Bid Whist is no exception to the rule. Although luck and the laws of random distribution have an impact, there is no substitute for decent player skills. Players without good skills may get an excellent hand and fail because they do not properly discard the Kitty, do not count the trumps, or do not make the correct bid initially.

Having the good fortune to find the right partner will also increase your winning percentage. This statement is somewhat misleading, however. The best partner for you may not be the player who appears to win the most games. Many believe that if they have a knowledgeable and experienced partner, then they will win every hand. This is often not true. I have seen many instances where two seemingly talented players play together and lose most of the night. You will find your best partner is the player who complements your style of play. When two players are synched in

---

[70] (Case's Online, n.d.) statistics captured for overall competition of each player

their approach to the game, they can become almost unbeatable.

It has been my experience that when two overly aggressive players are on the same team, one of them usually overbids. Teams of two passive players often underbid or pass and open the door for cheap No Trump bids. The strongest teams of Bid Whist players are two players who easily adapt to each other during the game. Each of the players is very capable of being the star player, but they allow their partner to be the leader as the game dictates. These team partnerships will usually be very successful.

CHAPTER SIXTEEN

Memorable Moments While Playing Bid Whist
An Early Birthday Gift

On one particular occasion, my team was in the hole, and our opponents bid five No Trump. Our deficit position left us no alternative than to pass. The bidder announced the direction as Uptown, and I feared the worst because I had only one face card, and I was missing an entire suit. The bidder's first card was the nine of Hearts, which was my missing suit. I showed a Club because my only face card was the King of Clubs. My partner won the Heart book with the Jack and played a Club. The bidder won with the Ace of Clubs and played the King of Hearts. My partner won the book with the Ace, and again played another Club, which I won and set the bid.

Normally this would not be very memorable, except we later learned that the bidder did not understand that he only had two losers in his hand. The bidder had nine Hearts, with the King and Queen and three Aces. There were only four Hearts not held by the bidder. My partner only had two Hearts, the Ace and Jack. If the bidder had played his King, then he would not have lost any more books. My partner and I were happy to be the benefactor of the bidder's generosity, but most players hate to see anyone misplay an excellent hand.

Making Seven with One Ace

Bid Whist is a challenging game with many twists and turns. I remember one game that was no exception. I did not have any decent hands for most of the night. My partner and I were four in the hole, and the other team had a score of four. I was the dealer and the first opponent bid three No Trump, and my partner passed. The 3rd position player bid five Downtown. I had The Big Joker, but I had no other card under a seven. I held the following cards:

BJ ♣KQJ1087, ♥K9, ♠K ♦KQ.

I knew that I could turn one book, but nothing else. My partner had passed, so in desperation, I bid six Uptown in Clubs, and the Kitty held: LJ ♠AQJ, ♣9, and ♥2.

I played my two Jokers, and the Ace of Clubs fell on the second Joker. My King and Queen captured the remaining trumps, and I was on my way to a Boston. I learned afterwards that my partner also had no low cards. If I had passed, the opponents would have made a Boston Downtown.

Luck of the Irish

There was one occasion when I had to place a protective bid with no cards of substance. I had absolutely nothing, and I placed a defensive bid of five Downtown. I got three aces out of the Kitty, which still left me with no anticipation of making the bid. After discarding the Kitty, my hand contained ♣456710KQ, ♥A, ♠A78 ♦A.

My first lead was the ♣4 and the 2nd position played the ♣3.

My partner then played the ♣2, and the 4th position played a Joker. Even with this unusual capture of some key cards, I had three losers still out. The opponents played Hearts, and I won with the Ace. I then played the ♣5, and the 2nd position player played the ♣A. My partner followed suit, and the 4th position player played the other Joker. That player again played Hearts, and I cut. Now I have the best trumps, but I still have two losers. I decided to take a chance. As I was sure the 4th position player had no trumps and I surmised my partner had the outstanding trump, I played my other two Aces and then played my ♣Q. My partner won with the ♣9 and had two winners, allowing me to discard my losing Spades. Such is the luck of the cards as we went from having no Jokers, no Aces, and no strong trumps, to making the bid.

Luck Will Always Change

Bid Whist is a game that features many twists and turns. There was a game where I had the ♣AKQJ3, ♥A, ♠J93 and my partner had the ♦AKQ. Now this would seem like a natural No Trump Uptown for our side. However, the opposing team bid six Uptown in Hearts. They ran a Boston because they caught my Ace and proceeded to run the Spades Uptown. Our team had three Aces and never turned one.

There Will Sometimes be Bumps in the Road

Another unusual turnaround happened when I was playing cards in one of the better-known spots in Chicago frequented by top-notch card players. Everyone's attention focused on a game between four very talented players. There was a lot of friendly trash talking and a sizable side bet on the game. The first two players passed, and the 3rd position player bid five Downtown. The dealer bid six Uptown and named Diamonds trump. After the player looked at the Kitty, he announced the bid was undefeatable and began to boast. The bidder had in his hand BJ, LJ, ♦AKQ, ♠AKQJ1072. People were looking over the shoulders of this player, and quietly agreeing that, yes, the game was over.

Now strangely, the player in 3rd position challenged the statement. They make a sizeable side bet on the outcome of the hand. Most of us around the table were gasping with amazement at this player throwing away his money. As the playing of the hand began, the mystery began to unfold. After the first book, it turns out only two players had trumps—the two who were involved in the betting. The bidder still felt very confident as he continued to play all of his trumps. I do not believe he ever counted the trumps, or he would have realized he was about to go over the cliff without a parachute.

The bidder hit all his trumps and played his Ace of Spades. The 3rd position player quickly cut the Spade book. The player not only set the bid, but, with the King of Hearts from his partner, they turned all the rest of the books. It turned out that the opponent had ♦J10987643, and knew no one had more trumps than he did. Well, that was the talk of the club for the next few days. In addition, it again proves that bad distribution will decimate even the best of hands.

Stay Out of your Partner's Lane

Always remember not to block your partner's run suit, especially if you cannot get back to your partner. While playing one game, I bid five No Trump in 1st position with three Aces. My hand was Uptown with ♥A367KQ, ♦AK9, ♣4, ♠A2. Surprisingly, my partner bid six No Trump and went Downtown. I was confident because my partner was Downtown. I knew my partner must have the Ace of Clubs.

My partner began to play Clubs as I had surmised. I had two Clubs with the four. My partner played the Ace and deuce and caught my four, and it became apparent that only my partner and the East position had Clubs. My partner hit the three of Clubs, and I showed a Heart, hoping my partner had the deuce. My partner broke a Heart, and I played the three and played back the Ace. I hoped my partner's hand contained three Hearts; however, when I played the Ace, my partner fell with the deuce, and this left the four of Hearts out there. I could only hope my partner had it, so I continued with the Hearts, but the East player had the four of Hearts.

East got in and played two more Clubs. My partner later complained that I should have played all my winners while I was in the hand. My partner failed to realize that even if I turned my two Hearts and my other three books, we would only have nine books, still two short of the required eleven books.

Perhaps if my partner had led the deuce of Hearts, things would have been different. I would have let that card go and waited for another Heart. Then I could play Hearts twice and catch the four of Hearts. We would have turned all five of the Hearts, plus the two Aces and deuce of Spades.

The moral of this story is when your hands shut down, cash in all your winners, and hope your partner can carry the rest of the hand. Another takeaway might be that when your partner has won the bid with a No Trump, and you have an Ace in your hand, why not let your partner play their hand. My partner scolded me because he bid six No Trump, and he only turned three books—Go Figure!

Lady Luck Frowns on Bad Playing

Earlier, I discussed the importance of being coordinated with your partner. An example is the story of a game when my partner bid three No Trump from the 2nd position after the opener passed. The 3rd position player bid four Downtown, and I followed with a four No Trump. I had ♣KJ1098765, ♥KQ9, ♠A. I led the Jack of Clubs and the player to my left played the Ace immediately, and led Spades. I played the Ace and led the King of Hearts. I knew my partner had either the Ace of Diamonds, the Ace of Hearts or both. My partner played the Ace on my King and began to run Diamonds. I showed a Club on the first Diamond book.

My partner played the A, K, and Q of Diamonds and played another Diamond even though my partner saw I never had a Diamond. The opponents turned the Diamond and then ran five Spades. We later reviewed the cards. We had all the Aces, the A, K, Q of Diamonds, and the A, K, Q of Hearts, plus the Ace of Spades. This should have been a virtual road map, but the inattention of my partner left us defeated for the bid. My partner could have played back a Heart or Club. Instead, he played a non-winning Diamond. It was a very frustrating defeat because the bid was makeable.

A Most Amorous Game

Another story with humor and romantic overtones occurred during a match at a Chicago nightspot. Lady Kathy, an attractive and talented Bid Whist player, bid a six No Trump. Now during these matches in taverns, the decorum can be rather relaxed, and trash talking can be very loud and entertaining. Kathy picked up her Kitty and, looking disgusted, threw the entire Kitty back without using any cards from it. As she prepared to play her first card, one of her male opponents announced the game was over and that Kathy could never make the bid. He stated that he was surprised at her making an outlandish bid such as a six No Trump. Kathy smiled sheepishly and said, "I might make it; I thought I had a chance."

The man stated, "You have no chance, and if you make this, I will buy you drinks for a month." Now this man had always admired and desired Kathy, so he put an ad-on to his bet. "If I set you, then tonight you are mine—all night." Kathy said, "That's a bet!" The fellow announced to the bartender, "Prepare my tab because Kathy and I are leaving in a few minutes." By then, everyone was laughing and coming over to see the game. The man showed his hand to the onlookers, and all were surprised that he had three Aces. Kathy began her play with the Ace of Spades, and then she proceeded to play many Spades. Well, the short of the story is that Kathy had eleven Spades. Not only did she make the bid, she made a Boston because the player did not know what to hold for the last card, and he threw away the Ace of Hearts and Ace of Diamonds. Alas, Kathy's final card was the deuce of Diamonds, and she made a Boston. There were plenty of laughs and free drinks for the next month in the club.

Lady Luck Will Occasionally Visit

Humor always abounds in the game of Bid Whist, and hilarious moments happen almost every night. There was one game where the player bid four Downtown and named Diamonds trumps. Apparently, his hand was almost two suited, with Clubs and Diamonds. The player got four Clubs out of the Kitty, with the Ace, deuce, and three. He got so excited with the Clubs that he threw away all of his Diamonds but the Ace, leaving himself with both Jokers, the Ace of Diamonds and nine Clubs. Lady Luck protects us sometimes because the opponents only had two Diamonds apiece, and his partner had four Diamonds. They made a Boston because after he hit his three trumps, his partner held the only trump left in the game.

It Looked Like a Ray Charles Hand

One of my favorite stories would be the time when in a game the dealer dealt himself one of the most unbelievable hands imaginable. He gasped in astonishment when he saw his cards. He began to show the hand to onlookers and smiled and said, "This game is OVER. This is a Boston!" His opponent stated, "I bet you cannot make a Boston with the hand you have now without using the Kitty cards." The dealer bet one hundred dollars that he could make a Boston. With the bet confirmed, the opponent immediately bid seven No Trump. He then stated, "You can't over-bid me, so you can't make a Boston, and I would appreciate you paying me with one big bill, please!"

Not All that Glitters is Gold

One of my funniest stories happened just before I finished this book, and I must include it in this list of funny things. It occurred when I was playing online. My partner and I were one-on, and the other team was five-in. My partner bid three Downtown and the second player passed. I do not remember all of my cards, but I know I had the Ace, five, and three of Hearts and three Diamonds to the Queen. I was afraid of a No Trump so I bid five Downtown as a defensive bid, hoping we might turn two books. The dealer passed, and I named Hearts as trump. My partner's bid indicated he held a Joker, and I was hoping to get a couple of Hearts out of the Kitty; after all that was my best suit. Well, the Kitty came with five Spades and the Ace of Diamonds. So now, I am stuck with my three trumps, eight Spades, Ace of Diamonds, and the deuce of Clubs.

Now in my mind, I know I cannot make this bid, so I played a big Spade first. The north player played the Ace, and my partner cut the book! My partner played the Ace of Clubs, and I played the deuce of Clubs. My partner then played the Diamonds, and I played my Ace. I then began to play my Spades, and my partner was throwing away Clubs. After I had played the third Spade, the north player accused us of cheating and stated he was forfeiting the game. The player then proceeded to quit the game.

My partner and I were upset at the accusation of cheating.

I was not upset for long because I was laughing so hard at the strange turn of events. Now I do not know what other cards my partner had to this day, but it was hilarious that we even had a chance to make a bid with that hand. I do not believe I could ever have made the bid because I only had three trumps, but I was going to try to cut with all three of them. My partner would have had to turn the rest of the books because I had nothing else. Even though it was a forfeit, how many players can say they made a bid with three trumps and no Joker? Moreover, who is to say that my partner would not have turned four or five books? Well, we will never know, and the funniest part of all this is that I do believe we would have been set except for the anger of the player who gave us the forfeit.

Dog Day Afternoon

I have many wonderful memories of laughable moments that occurred during Bid Whist games. One of my personal, humorous stories was not very funny at the time. It happened on a Saturday afternoon gathering of neighborhood Bid Whist players at the Katanga Lounge on Chicago's Westside. Afternoon games are common for many taverns because it avoids interference with the tavern's evening party patrons.

The Saturday afternoon games at the taverns were like indoor picnics. The gatherings were small, casual, and very relaxed. The tavern owner provided sandwiches and snacks. The Katanga Lounge was an older tavern, and like most of the aged Chicago taverns, it had an adjacent room to handle any overflow patrons on busy nights. The adjoining rooms of the taverns had large entranceways and did not have doors, to allow for easy access and visibility to the main tavern area. The Katanga Lounge was an antique dealer's dream because it had many small stained-glass windows, authentic mahogany woodwork on the bar and seating booths, and one of the original wooden Bell telephone booths with a working rotary dial telephone.

On this afternoon, the tavern owner's oldest son, Ricky, stopped by to drop off bar supplies in preparation for the Saturday night crowd. His pet pedigreed Rottweiler accompanied Ricky. He walked the dog into the adjoining room and secured the dog to a steel exit door in the room. A couple of the card players assisted Ricky with bringing in the bar supplies. A few minutes later, Ricky found there were missing items that required a return to the bar supply store.

Ricky went back to the supply store, and we continued with our Bid Whist game. I had terrible hands all afternoon, until Lady Luck finally tapped me on the shoulder. I had the most amazing hand I had ever seen, and have never seen again. Many players have caught remarkable hands and achieved a Boston with the help of the Kitty or their partner. I had the Bid Whist Players' dream, as I had received the "Perfect Hand."[71] I did not need the Kitty nor my partner—I held a Boston! I do not remember the bidding order, but I did not have first bid, and I was salivating waiting for

---

[71] A hand containing eight trumps that outrank all other trumps and the four highest-ranking cards of another suit, or an optional No Trump hand containing the three highest-ranking cards in all four suits.

the bid to get to me, so I could bid SEVEN.

You may have guessed by now, but Lady Luck left as quickly as she appeared. Before I had the opportunity to bid, pandemonium broke out in the tavern. I heard screaming and the sound of breaking glass. I saw cards thrown in the air and people quickly running through the tavern for the door. I saw two men run into the wooden telephone booth, and others were either standing on tables or jumping on the bar. The Rottweiler was loose! I dropped my cards and ran with others to jump on the bar.

Ricky's stepfather, W.C., apparently had gone to feed the dog, and the dog's collar had slipped from its neck. W.C. was 6'2", 240 lbs., and upon finding himself holding the leash and collar with no dog, he leaped quickly into action. W.C. dove for the dog and caught this enormous animal in a headlock with his left arm. I can still vividly remember W.C. sprawled on the floor with the dog in the grip of his left arm while he tried to replace the collar on the dog's head with his right hand. The Rottweiler weighed well over 120 lbs., and W.C. was probably the only person in the tavern that could have accomplished this feat.

This all occurred in the span of two to three minutes, but afterwards, W.C. was exhausted and dripping with perspiration. The tavern was in disarray, as people slowly came down from their perches, the washrooms, and other places of hiding. It took a while to get things cleaned up, and the tables and chairs up-righted. The two men who had fled into the telephone booth were stuck in the phone booth! It took several minutes to get them out because of the interruptions of laughter at the many Superman anecdotes. The playing cards from the game were scattered across the floor, and my anticipated moment of glory had gone to the dogs. I have never again had such a strong opening hand dealt to me.

EPILOGUE

I hope you have enjoyed reading this information as much as I enjoyed putting it together for fellow avid Bid Whist players. My focus was to establish the rich background of this enjoyable game that has become a treasured part of African American culture. The game continues to evolve both here in the United States and in many countries abroad.

This research project gave me an immense sense of Black pride. I discovered an invisible thread connecting my life with you the reader, the former slaves, and many amazing Black people. Our commonalities of slave ancestors, skin color, and struggles to overcome, have often been bundled and tied together by the threads of Bid Whist.

I hope that this writing has provided you some insights on Bid Whist game strategies. These strategies follow the random percentage probabilities and distribution odds. However, I think you will agree that with all things being equal, nothing can beat luck. I have found that luck is usually a close friend to those players with talent and good skills. If you play your hands poorly, your luck will run badly. I encourage readers to develop their basic skills and game knowledge, and allow luck to have an open invitation at the table.

The ideas and strategies I have shared in this book can help you to triumph at Bid Whist more consistently. They will also help you increase your overall winning percentages. I wish for you four Aces and two Jokers on each hand.

"Life is not always a matter of holding good cards, but sometimes playing a poor hand well." —Jack London, undated.

GLOSSARY

Bean Town—term that describes a team winning the game by turning all the books played during that particular hand. This is another term used for a "Boston."

Beat down—a term describing a team suffering a significant and decisive loss.

Bid—the declaration of the number of books (over six) a team expects to make during a hand.

Book— single round of play consisting of the playing of one card from each player—also called a TRICK.

Booked Card—a card turned face up in the deck with its suit and rank visible to the players.

Boston—slang term used to describe a team turning all the books on a bid to win the game. This slang is believed to have been coined by the Pullman porters who worked on the train that went straight through to Boston, the term thereby meaning going all the way to the last stop. If a team turns every book without winning the game, the term used is "7 cards."

Cards have Backs on Them—expression used by players meaning that cards in a player's hand are unexposed cards and therefore an unknown quantity. Players used this term when they did not know which card or suit was appropriate to play.

Church is Out—the game is finished and the team has won.

Custer's Last Stand—a player in 1st position holding a mediocre hand, and making a very high No Trump bid with very little overall support to back up the chances of making the bid.

Cut—player wins a book by playing a trump card on a book of another suit.

Cut the Deck—player must divide the deck into two separate sections and re-form the deck by switching the positions of the two sections.

Deal—the dealer distributes one card at a time to each player until the deck is fully distributed.

Deck—combination of all the cards of the four suits plus the Big and Little Jokers.

Deuce—the term used for the numeral two.

Downtown—play of the cards reversed in ranking order so that the lowest cards have dominance. The rank moves consecutively from the Ace (highest rank) downwardly to the King (lowest rank).

Even Board—term used for whenever a team has a board score of zero.

Finesse—a player holding the Ace or other higher winning card plays another card, hoping to turn two books in the suit.

Glossary

Going out Backwards—a team making a bid that will cause them to lose the game if the bid is set.

Half Steppin'—slang term that indicates the game allows Downtown bids to outrank any Uptown bids of the same numerical level. There are regions that do not permit half-steppin', and the player is required to bid six Downtown to overbid a five Uptown.

Heavy—term used to indicate a partner who frequently passes, or is reluctant to bid and is not carrying his load as a team member.

In the Hole—a team has a negative board score that is under zero.

Kitty—six cards are dealt and placed to the side at the beginning of each hand. The player with the highest bid wins these six cards.

Lead—the first card played in a trick.

Lead Away—player in the 1st position holding the best card leads a lesser card in an attempt to turn two books in that suit—also known as a Finesse.

Low—the lowest cards of the suit will have ranking dominance.

Money—when a takeout bid might be necessary, the team has a score high enough to make the required bid without going out backwards. The points can be "spent" when necessary as a defensive move.

On Board—a team has a positive board score above zero.

Pat Hand—holding a hand in which each of a player's cards is dominant over any of the cards held by the other players.

Playing out of turn—a player places his card on the table before the player in front of him plays his card.

Phone Numbers—player's hand in which all the cards range from three to nine, with no winners or significant pushers.

Pop—slang for a bid of seven Uptown (Seven-Up).

Pusher—a player holds a card that forces the playing of the best card in a suit. A King or deuce has the ability to force the playing of the Ace, or the Little Joker can push a player to play the Big Joker.

Revoke or Renege—the play of a card of another suit by a player who is able to follow suit.

Rise and Shine or Rise and Fly—the losing team must give up their seats to new players.

Road Map—hand that is virtually undefeatable at the bid level announced. The player possesses the cards that will enable that player to make the bid without any help from their partner.

Rubber—term indicating a best of three games match which ends when one team wins two games. When both teams have won one game each, the last game is the Rubber Game.

Sharp Top—slang term for the Ace.

Showing a Card—when a player runs out of a suit, the player discards a card to indicate he has a possible winner in the suit.

Skate—the player in the 2nd or 3rd position with the best card in the suit attempts to win the trick by playing the third or fourth best card, hoping the second best card is in front of the player to win two books from the suit.

Sluff—a player's first discard when they can no longer follow suit.

Smell the Tea—slang phrase for a Boston is on the way.

Special—a term describing the cards of a suit played with the lowest cards having dominance. A part of the original Bid Whist lingo used by people in the southern regions.

Sporting the Kitty—the revealing of the hidden cards that were placed on the table as the Kitty.

Suit—one of the four categories within a deck of cards, Hearts, Diamonds, Clubs, or Spades--a suit consists of thirteen cards from one of these denominations, ranging from the Ace downward to the deuce.

Sweep—a team wins all the games in a match.

Throw-off—when a suit that a player does not possess is put on board, and that player does not cut but instead discards, losing cards of another suit. This usually occurs when a player runs out of trumps or when the player's partner is playing winning cards that do not require the player to cut.

Trey—slang for the numeral three.

Trick— the playing of one card from each player, also called a Book.

Trump—any card of the suit named as the ranking suit by the winning bidder. The lowest trump card will beat any card from another suit, regardless of rank.

Trump-Tight—the remaining cards in a player's hands are all trumps.

Twins—term used to indicate possessing a combination of both the Big and Little Jokers.

Uptown—the play of the cards in ranking order with the highest cards having dominance.

Whisk—word meaning whisking up a trick with one of the four cards. Player would take the winning card, place under the other cards, and scoop the other three cards in a motion similar to sweeping up dirt. Many believe it was the origin of the word Whist.

Window Cleaning—team completes two consecutive matches by winning all the games.

Wolf Tickets—slang phrase for bluffing.

BIBLIOGRAPHY

A Brief History of Playings Cards. (2007). Retrieved from US Playing Card Co.: http://web.archive.org/web/20070826144858/http://www.usplayingcard.com/gamerules/briefhistory.html.

Agee, R. W. (1981). How to Play Bid Whist. Library of Congress Registration# TX0002476312.

Ainslie, F.-L. C. (n.d.). *The Principles and practice of Whist.*

Albert Morehead, R. L.-S. (1964). *The New Complete Hoyle.* Garden City Books.

American whist League. (1891). *The laws of whist as adopted by the first American Whist congress.* Ithaca: Journal book and commercial printing house.

Andrews, J. D. (2001). *The complete win at whist.* Chicago: Bonus Books.

Andrews, J. (n.d.). *YouTube.* Retrieved from http://www.youtube.com/watch?v=OR9xAXAA-N8 Joe Andrews

Bailey, G. W. (1885). *A Handbook of Whist.*

Beck, A. C. (1994). *How to play bid whist: you can't play without a partner.* Stamford, CT: Zwita Productions.

Burney, J. (1821). *An essay, by way of lecture on the game of whist.* London: Library of Congress LC#28010152.

Cady, A. H. (1895). *Whist, a brief history of the game.* New York: American sports publishing co.

Case's Online. (n.d.). Retrieved from CLO Bid Whist: http://www.igl.net/clobidwhist

Coffin, C. E. (1895). *The gist of whist.* New York, Chicago: Brentano's.

Current Validated Living Supercentenarians. (2014, May). Retrieved from Gerontology Research Group: http://www.grg.org/Adams/E.HTM

Dick, W. B. (1884). *Dick's Handbook of Whist.*

Fitch, G. (1910). *Bridge Whist.*

Fitch, G. (1910). *Bridge Whist.*

Foster, R. F. (1898). *Foster's Common Sense in Whist.*

Franklin, E. (2001). *The Killing Table: An African American Icon.*

Greg Morrison, Y. R. (2005). *Rise and fly: tall tales and mostly true rules of bid whist.* New York: Three Rivers Press.

Hempl, G. (1887). *Whist scores and card-table talk, with a Bibliography of Whist.*

Hoyle, E. (1743). *A short treatise on the game of whist.* London: W. Webster.

Johnson, H. (2003). *Bid Whist: The Making of a Great American Pastime.*

Jones, C. (2013). *How to master Bid Whist.*

Keiley, C. (1859). *The laws and practice of whist.*

KRTApps. (n.d.). Bid Whist.

Library of Congress. (n.d.). Off-duty porters playing whist http://hdl.loc.gov/loc.pnp/cph.3b23118.

Bibliographies

Matthews, P. J. (1981, 11 09). Guide to straight and bid whist. Library of Congress Registration #TX00000807160.

Moyer, F. E. (1903). *Whist things old and new.*

Myers, R. a. (2005). *Remembering the Path to T-Town: Migration of an African American Family through Seven States to Lincoln, Nebraska.* Washington, DC: RJMPUB Publishers.

National Bid Whist Association. (n.d.). *Tournament Rules.* Retrieved from nationalbidwhist.org: http://nationalbidwhist.org/tournamentrules.php

Ostrow, A. A. (1951). *The Complete Card Player.*

Pettes, G. W. (1886). *American or Standard Whist.*

Pettes, G. W. (1887). *Whist Universal.*

Poole, W. (1895). *The Evolution of Whist.*

Richards, J. (1889). *A new method of playing and scoring Whist.*

Robertson, E. (. (1902). *The Roberston rule and other axioms of bridge whist.* New York: Press of "Bollettino della sera."

Rules of Card Games: Bid Whist. (n.d.). Retrieved from Pagat.com: http://www.pagat.com

Shaw, M. (1898). *Nine Thousand miles on a Pullman Train.* Allen, Lane, and Scott.

Ship, D. J. (n.d.). *Bid Whist.* Retrieved from pagat.com: http://www.pagat.com

The Legacy of Pullman Porters. (n.d.). Retrieved from http://www.museumoftheamericanrailroad.org/Resources/TheLegacyofPullmanPorters.aspx

Thomas, B. (1993). *Finally--rules on bid whist*. Atlanta: Thomas Publishing Co. of CARDJAZZ.

Tye, L. (2007). *Rising from the Rails: Pullman Porters and the Making of the Black Middle* Owl.

www.whistportal.com. (n.d.). Retrieved from Whistportal: http://www.whistportal.com/

http://en.wikipedia.org/wiki/Pullman_Company

http://www.youtube.com/watch?v=OR9xAXAA-N8   Joe Andrews

About the Publisher

Let us bring your story to life! With Life to Legacy, we offer the following publishing services: manuscript development, editing, transcription services, ghostwriting, cover design, copyright services, ISBN assignment, worldwide distribution, and eBooks.

Throughout the entire production process, you maintain control over your project. We are here to serve you. Even if you have no manuscript at all, we can ghostwrite your story for you from audio recordings or legible handwritten documents.

We also specialize in family history books, so you can leave a written legacy for your children, grandchildren, and others. You put your story in our hands, and we'll bring it to literary life! We have several publishing packages to meet all your publishing needs.

Call us at: 877-267-7477, or you can also send e-mail to: Life2Legacybooks@att.net. Please visit our Web site:

www.Life2Legacy.com

www.ingramcontent.com/pod-product-compliance
Lightning Source LLC
Chambersburg PA
CBHW021334090426
42742CB00008B/605